Pub. Feb. 13 1797 by H. Humphrey New Bond Street
Js. Gy. inv. & fec.
AL-BOWER; _with the Evil-One, peeping at the Charms of Eden.
from Milto

BRITISH PRIME MINISTERS

PITT THE YOUNGER

OVERLEAF
William Pitt the Younger
by Gainsborough.

PITT THE YOUNGER

DEREK JARRETT

INTRODUCTION BY
A. J. P. TAYLOR

WEIDENFELD AND NICOLSON
LONDON

Designed by Karen Bowen
for George Weidenfeld and Nicolson Ltd
11 St John's Hill, London SW11 1XA

Filmset and printed Offset Litho by
Cox & Wyman Ltd
London, Fakenham and Reading

ISBN 0 297 76668 6

CONTENTS

PREFACE

THOSE WHO TREAT HISTORY as the handmaiden of politics have always made great play with the younger Pitt, seeing him as the prophet of this or that nineteenth-century movement, the enemy of this or that twentieth-century aspiration. For the working historian, however, he is none of these things. He is a product of the eighteenth-century political scene: worldly, aristocratic and with very few illusions about the wickedness and weakness of mankind. This book tries to put him back into his proper context; and the starting point of any such attempt must of course be the work of the late Sir Lewis Namier, who did more than any other historian to recapture for us the flavour and the nuances of late eighteenth-century politics. I have been fortunate in being able to discuss my work with some of Namier's colleagues and in particular with John Brooke, to whom I owe a very great deal. I have also received help from scholars working in the field of nineteenth-century history, especially from my friend and colleague Dr W.H.C. Smith. Other colleagues and pupils, not only at Goldsmiths' College but throughout the University of London, have provided stimulus and assistance. This little book may prove too slight to merit the kindnesses I have received, but at least it may be allowed to serve as a vehicle for my gratitude.

J.D.J. *London, 1973*

ACKNOWLEDGMENTS

Photographs were supplied by, or are reproduced by kind permission of the following: the picture on page 18 by gracious permission of H.M. The Queen; Barclays Bank Ltd., Cambridge: 87; Brighton Art Gallery: 61; British Museum: 16–17, 20, 44, 88–9, 93/2, 104, 116/2, 134/2, 138–9, 140, 145, 148/1, 148/2, 149, 171, 179, 194–5, 198, 215; Cambridge University Library: 31; Courtauld Institute of Art: 13; Department of the Environment (Crown Copyright): 143, 200–1; Mary Evans Picture Library: 35, 74, 99, 120–1, 128–9, 173, 174; John Freeman: 40–1, 155; The Grenville Trustees: 29; Library of Congress: 117; The Honourable Society of Lincoln's Inn: 42, 59; London Museum: 43, 68, 69, 100; Mansell Collection: 24–5, 38–9, 46/1, 49, 54, 55, 63, 80–1, 83, 85, 91, 106–7, 111, 113, 118, 122, 123, 134/1, 160–1, 162, 164–5, 167, 168, 170, 176–7, 191, 193, 206, 207/1, 207/2, 212–13; National Library of Ireland: 96–7, 184–5; National Maritime Museum: 210–11; National Monuments Record: 37; National Museum of Wales: 93/1; National Portrait Gallery: 11/2, 38, 39, 70, 76, 203; Master and Fellows, Pembroke College, Cambridge: 11/1; Photo Hachette: 65; Tate Gallery: 32–3; Victoria and Albert Museum: 46/2, 98, 133, 148–9; Weidenfeld and Nicolson: 116/1, 152, 205; Librarian and Curator, Borough of Yeovil: 22–3.

Picture research by Andra Nelki.

INTRODUCTION

THE YOUNGER PITT has a special place among prime ministers for many reasons. He was the youngest of them all. He held the office without a break for longer than any of his successors. He was also the only prime minister, unless one counts Neville Chamberlain, who owed his appointment as much to his father's name as to his own abilities. These abilities were great. He was an orator of the first rank, his phrases shaped like passages of Latin prose. He had considerable administrative gifts and some understanding of finance. Most of all he inherited from his father an aptitude for power. He was the first prime minister to dominate his cabinet. He dominated the House of Commons. Even extreme incompetence as a war minister did not shake his position, and he became after his death the symbol of British resistance to Napoleon.

Pitt had plenty to show for his long term of office. He devised a system for British rule in India that lasted for seventy years. He invented the income tax which is still with us almost unchanged. He carried the union with Ireland, the lamentable consequences of which are also still with us. He conducted a long war against revolutionary France that is regarded by some as heroic and by others as a catastrophe for both Europe and this country. Yet his constitutional position was curious. George III chose him as prime minister, and he in return rescued the King from dictation by a political party.

Pitt began as a Whig and always claimed to hold Whig principles. His legacy was the second Tory party, the party of repression and reaction. The legacy was a confused one. Those who applauded the massacre of Peterloo drank to the immortal memory of Mr Pitt. So did the moderate efficient men who began the process of reform. Sir Robert Peel was beyond dispute a Pittite, and Peel's greatest disciple was Gladstone. It is safer to say that Pitt stood above party, relying on his own achievements and the great shadow of Chatham. In a way he was the first of the prime ministers who ruled in the interest of the possessing class and yet called themselves national leaders – a position acceptable in wartime and otherwise tawdry.

Pitt did not stand alone in grandeur. Charles James Fox was an antagonist whose name will always be linked with his. Fox was as long out of office as Pitt was in. Fox was gay and dissolute, where Pitt was austere and, except for his drinking habits, respectable. Fox preached allegiance to party. Pitt served George III. Richard Pares wrote: 'Though George III won the present, Fox won the future.' It was Fox, not Pitt, who shaped the modern British constitution. On the greatest questions of the age – the war against France and the suppression of the British liberties – Fox, in my opinion, was absolutely right and Pitt was absolutely wrong. Derek Jarrett has judiciously presented the story of Pitt's enormously important career. It is a career in which I find much to admire, if, personally, little to like.

A.J.P.TAYLOR

I

FATHER AND SON

On 22 February 1766 William Pitt the elder, formerly chief minister to King George II and soon to be chief minister again under his successor, wrote home exultantly to tell his wife and children about a great victory which he and his political associates had just won in the House of Commons. They had secured the repeal of the notoriously unpopular American Stamp Act and they were confident that in doing so they had averted the danger of a revolt in America. From 1757 to 1761 Pitt had been a brilliantly successful war minister, presiding over the conquest from the French of vast areas of North America; and many people had come to think of him as in effect the creator of Britain's enormous and unwieldy empire on the other side of the Atlantic. His critics pointed out, with some measure of truth, that his conquests had made relations between colonists and the mother country worse rather than better: landed men in England felt that they were being taxed to the hilt merely to make more money for colonial merchants, while the colonists themselves were increasingly reluctant to pay their share of the costs of empire now that the defeat of the French had made them less dependent on London for protection. But Pitt's admirers swept aside such arguments as impatiently as they swept the Stamp Act itself from the Statute Book. As far as they were concerned Pitt was the friend and champion not only of the freedom-loving Americans but of freedom itself. He had forged an empire of free men, defeating the tyranny and absolutism of France to do so, and now he would defend that same empire and its freedoms from the tyranny of King George III's misguided ministers.

Pitt's most enthusiastic and most valued admirers were to be found in the bosom of his own family. His home was a haven of hero-worship, a place where he could always be sure of adulation even at times when politicians and party leaders turned against him. He had married Lady Hester Grenville, sister of two of his closest political associates, in the autumn of 1754. Their first child, a daughter who was also called Hester, arrived in the following year. She was followed by John in 1756, Harriot in 1758 and William Pitt the younger in 1759. A third son, James Charles, was born in 1761. He was destined to bear somewhat sad witness to his father's lifelong concern for seapower and for the Caribbean trade by dying of disease in the West Indies in 1780 as a nineteen-year-old naval captain. John, as eldest son, was marked out to be the

PREVIOUS PAGE RIGHT A drawing from Pembroke College, Cambridge, which may represent young William Pitt.
LEFT William Pitt the Elder, Earl of Chatham.

Lady Hester Grenville,
Pitt's mother, by T. Hudson.

stallion of the family, the boy whose chief business it was to beget children and ensure the continuance of the family name and the family estates. But there was never any doubt that it was to his second son and namesake that the great William Pitt looked for the perpetuation of his political ideals. 'Eager Mr William', as he came to be called, was born on 28 May 1759, at the opening of that phenomenal campaigning season which was later to be dubbed 'the Year of Victories'. Pitt's countrymen were to remember it as the year that brought the scattering of the French navy, the conquest of Canada and India, the crumbling of French power in theatres of war as far apart as Germany and the West Indies. For Pitt himself it was also, perhaps most important of all, the year that had brought him his 'Sweet William'. And now, in his moment of triumph over the repeal of the Stamp Act, it was William's opinion and approbation that mattered.

The boy's mother was foolish enough to reply to her husband's letter without stopping to ascertain the reactions of his favourite child. Hester and John, she wrote, were 'by no means indifferent' to their father's success and she could add their congratulations to her own. But 'Eager Mr William', she reported somewhat apologetically, 'I have not yet seen'. The reply she received was genial enough but it had an edge to it which showed that the omission had been noted and regretted. 'Loves to the sweet babes, patriotic or not,' the statesman wrote, 'though I hope impetuous William is not behind in feelings of that kind.' Later, when William had reached the mature age of seven years, his father made it clear that he was expected to have appropriate political opinions as well as appropriate patriotic feelings. 'I expect many sage reflections from William upon the public papers,' declared a paternal letter of July 1766.

There was of course a certain amount of amused irony in all this, just as there was in the family habit of referring to young William as 'the Young Senator' or 'the Philosopher'. But there was also a fierce and very real pride, a jealous determination that the rising hope of the house of Pitt should be the wisest and most talented of children, able, as his mother once wrote, 'to enjoy with the greatest pleasure what would be above the reach of any other creature of his small age'. When a friend congratulated Pitt in 1763 on being at home 'surrounded by your pretty prattlers', he received a slightly sharp reply in which the statesman modulated the bantering reference into a somewhat different key, speaking of 'the diminutive philosophers who surround us'. The Pitt family circle was intensely self-absorbed and defensive, in small things as well as great. Just as it closed ranks around the head of the household when he was – or imagined himself to be – under attack from his fellow politicians, so it was quick to rebut any slight upon the dignity of its younger members. Pitts, however young, did not prattle.

Five months after the repeal of the Stamp Act, while young William was still no doubt studying to produce the 'sage reflections' which were required of him, the elder Pitt was called upon once again to be the chief minister of the King. Originally George III had been extremely suspicious of Pitt, disliking his lofty pretensions and deploring the 'bloody and expensive war' into which he seemed to have dragged the country. But now, six years after his accession, the idealistic young King saw that he had more in common with the lonely figure of Pitt than he had with most of the other politicians, party men for the most part, who were contending for his favour. In the King's eyes they were almost all rogues, using the party groupings which they controlled in the House of Commons in order to force themselves into office. Pitt, on the other hand, boasted constantly that he was 'single and unconnected' and that he championed honest and independent men – including of course the King himself, the most honest and independent of all – against the caballing party leaders. Every now and again Pitt's own rather unsavoury political manoeuvres were dragged into the light and he was discredited by the journalists he hired, by the party leaders he sought to manipulate or by the borough and city corporations which he controlled for political purposes. But for most of the time his reputation as the architect of victory, together with his awesome powers as an orator in the House of Commons, enabled him to be taken at his face value, as the one man in the kingdom who could heal party divisions and reconcile all social groups, from rebellious colonists in America to independent landed men in England, to the King's government. This he was now asked to do. George III, who had come to the throne determined to treat Pitt as the most untrustworthy of all the untrustworthy politicians with whom he had to deal, now swallowed his pride sufficiently to ask that same Pitt to form a new kind of ministry aimed at 'destroying all party distinction and restoring that subordination to government

OVERLEAF New Palace Yard, Westminster in the middle of the eighteenth century.

George III and Queen Charlotte with their children in 1770. Left to right, William, Duke of Clarence, George, Prince of Wales, Frederick, Duke of York, Princess Augusta, Princess Charlotte and Princess Elizabeth.

which can alone preserve that inestimable blessing Liberty from degenerating into Licentiousness'.

Pitt did indeed succeed in holding licentiousness at bay, but unfortunately he did not succeed in providing effective or even coherent government. Within less than a year his ministry was in ruins and his policies were the subject of public contempt and ridicule. He shut himself away from London and from political life, relying upon his wife to keep his colleagues from the door and to block their increasingly anxious inquiries as to how government was supposed to be carried on. For days on end he refused to see anybody at all and had his food left at a serving-hatch which he would not open until he was sure the servants had gone. This was the pitiable reality behind all the brave talk of non-party government. The enormous problems of the British empire and monarchy, problems which had already tested existing administrative techniques to the limit and had estranged the King from his ministers and the colonists from their home country, had been entrusted to the genius of one man; and the one man had broken under the strain.

Once before, at the opening of the war with the French in 1756, Pitt had said that he could save his country and that nobody else could. On that occasion he had kept his promise, turning defeat into victory and pushing the nation into uncharted and seemingly limitless seas of maritime expansion. But now the man who had built an empire seemed incapable of keeping it together; the politician who had smashed the old party cliques seemed unable to put anything in their place except the wordy grandeur of his own paranoia. After nearly two years of depression and apathy he rushed to the opposite extreme, resigning from his own ministry and then tearing it to pieces in a furious paroxysm of opposition. After that all activity ceased, even the frenzied alternation between mania and depression, and the elder Pitt passed into the long twilight of the 1770s, torturing himself and those around him with the unanswered and unanswerable questions. What had gone wrong? Why had the King whom he had tried to save returned to the bad old ways of corruption and unpopularity? Why had the empire he created been torn apart by revolution? Had he failed his country or had his country failed him?

There was only one person who could offer solace for the past or hope for the future, only one companion who would listen without complaint to the endless recriminations. Young William, who had until now been a means of escaping from a busy and fulfilled political life, a favourite child to be indulged on those infrequent occasions when the great statesman could find time 'to devote Saturday to children and to hay-making', now became the substitute and the consolation for a political life that had collapsed. For more than a decade, from the disintegration of his father's last ministry in the late 1760s to his father's death in May 1778, his own boyhood was overshadowed by the slow decline and final decrepitude of his father. Pitt the elder did not approve of public schools – boys were cowed for life at Eton, he once declared – and so William was subjected to an unremitting regime of home lessons and

A French view of the elder Pitt.

private tutors, behind which there stood the awe-inspiring and steadily more demented figure of his father. Some years later, when the young William Pitt became the King's chief minister at the age of twenty-four, his enemies produced some satirical verses suggesting that the government front bench in the House of Commons should be padded, lest the bare wood prove too hard for a youthful backside still scarred from school floggings. Their intention was doubly ironic, designed to point out that even as a schoolboy Pitt was deficient, having been coddled at home and 'taught by his dad on a stool' instead of being exposed to the bracing rigours of school life. They were soon to learn that the austere and lonely years of his boyhood had toughened him in ways undreamed of by the case-hardened advocates of the public school system.

Childhood's end for young William came some two months after his seventh birthday, while he was on holiday at Weymouth with his brothers and sisters in the summer of 1766. On their way there from Burton Pynsent, their father's country house in the north of Somerset, they had been greeted by the ringing of bells and other demonstrations of affection in the towns they passed through, as people came into the streets to honour the children of the nation's hero. Burton Pynsent itself was a symbol of that same honour and acclaim: it had been bequeathed to the elder Pitt by a complete stranger, Sir William Pynsent, in recognition of his services as 'the Great Commoner', the stalwart defender of ordinary Englishmen against the proud and corrupt noblemen who had controlled for so long the King's government and the two Houses of Parliament which were supposed to keep that government under their surveillance. Pitt had once described the House of Commons as 'a parcel of younger brothers' – younger brothers, that is, of the men who sat in the House of Lords. He was also the declared enemy of the jobbery and corruption which enabled noblemen to build up a commanding interest in certain boroughs and thus determine who should sit in the Commons as members for those boroughs.

Like Sir William Pynsent, the enthusiasts who rang their bells for the Pitt children seemed to forget that the Pitt family had its share of these so-called 'rotten boroughs' and that Pitt himself had once sat for one of them before moving to another, equally rotten, which had been provided for him by the Duke of Newcastle. On one occasion Pitt called Newcastle 'the wretch who draws the great families at his heels'; but this did not prevent him from utilising, when it suited him, the power structure which Newcastle and his noble friends inhabited. Like most members of the House of Lords, Newcastle was a Whig, a member of that political party which accepted the need for corruption as the only means of preserving the country's stability and safeguarding the Hanoverian kings against the possible return of the Stuarts. The Stuart kings

OVERLEAF Burton Pynsent, bequeathed to the elder Pitt in 1765 by Sir William Pynsent.

had had to go into exile during the previous century because their rule had seemed to threaten freedom and property – two things which were almost identical in England, since most property was freehold property and most freedoms could only be exercised by freeholders. While the Whigs insisted that freedom and property could be preserved only by means of a power structure which bound together all office-holders, both in government and in Parliament as a whole, in defence of the Hanoverian dynasty, Pitt and his friends claimed that this structure represented merely the Court and the aristocracy rather than the country as a whole. Therefore they tended to call themselves 'the Country Interest' or 'the Patriots' – representatives, that is, of the *patria* or fatherland – as opposed to the narrowly oligarchic Whigs. Sometimes they even experimented

Weymouth, where the Pitt children spent a summer holiday in 1766 and heard the news of their father's appointment as chief minister.

with the title 'Tory', traditionally the opposite of Whig, but this was somewhat dangerous because it suggested that they would welcome the return of the house of Stuart. Even at the end of the eighteenth century, when Pitt the younger had at last completed his father's work and ended the supremacy of the Whigs, his followers were still reluctant to take the final step and call themselves Tories.

The importance of the summer of 1766, both in the political life of the nation and in the personal life of young William Pitt, was that the emptiness of his father's 'Patriotic' and anti-aristocratic pretensions was suddenly and startlingly revealed. For at the end of July the five children holidaying at Weymouth learned not just that their father had accepted office but that he had also accepted a peerage. Their mother had for some

years been Lady Chatham in her own right, an honour which the elder Pitt had accepted from a grateful King and country in 1761 on retiring from his first ministry. At that time he had had the political good sense to refuse a peerage for himself, knowing full well that his championing of the country against the Whig oligarchy would look a little silly if it were carried on from within the House of Lords itself. Now, however, the attractions of a peerage proved too strong and he agreed to become the Earl of Chatham. His first ministry, the brilliantly successful administration in whose honour Burton Pynsent had been bequeathed and the bells of so many churches rung, had been led by a Great Commoner; but this one, so soon to become sadly inglorious, was under the command of a peer of the realm, a member of that same House of Lords whose powers and influence the Great Commoner had so sturdily opposed. It was left to a seven-year-old boy – 'the only surviving Mr William Pitt' as his tutor called him whimsically – to restore that image of the house of Pitt and of its political mission which his father had destroyed at a stroke by becoming the Earl of Chatham.

The shattering of the image had already been foreshadowed at Burton Pynsent, where the elder Pitt had been planning for many months alterations and extensions designed to turn the home of a simple country gentleman into a habitation fit for a great lord. And while the masons and carpenters tramped their dusty way about the great house, its owners turned to their respective concerns: the newly ennobled father to his designs for liveried servants and emblazoned carriages, the elder son to his dreams of eventual inheritance and the second son to his own more daunting legacy. It was his business to equip himself, in such schoolrooms and libraries as the chaos of rebuilding left available, for the task of rescuing and restoring the political reputation of the house of Pitt.

The basic equipment was the same as it was for any gentleman's son in the eighteenth century: a knowledge of the classical authors of Greece and Rome. William's tutors were staggered and almost awed by the rapid progress he made. He never seemed to learn, they reported, but only to recollect. He was equally at home with other subjects, such as history and mathematics and modern poetry, which were later added to the curriculum. Lady Holland, the mother of his future opponent Charles Fox, saw him when he was still only seven and declared that he was 'really the cleverest child I ever saw; and so strictly brought up and so proper in his behaviour that, mark my words, that little boy will be a thorn in Charles's side as long as he lives'. The cleverness was indeed phenomenal, but it was the strict upbringing, the constant and relentless demand that he should conform to adult standards, that really set him apart. It was not accompanied by the physical severities which he would have encountered if he had gone away to school, although on one occasion Chatham did apparently make him kneel down to be flogged by Hiley Addington, son of the family doctor, so that he should know what happened to the boys at Winchester.

Hiley Addington was William's exact contemporary and Henry, his elder brother, was two years older. They seem to have been almost the only children he played with, apart from his own brothers and sisters, and they apparently looked down on him at first as a puny and rather priggish individual who had not been toughened by life at Winchester as they had. Later their attitude changed and they came to share the general admiration for his astonishing charm and talents. There are many accounts of these talents but it should be remembered that they were all written by his elders: since he had no school-fellows and few playmates there is no way of knowing whether he ever really had time to be a boy before hurrying on to be, by his early teens, such a prodigious and poised adult. Some of his pleasures were those of boyhood – he rode and bathed and walked a lot, and he went bird's-nesting in the copses at Holwood, near his father's house in Kent – but it is usually through the eyes of adults that we see him enjoying them. 'It is a delight to see William see nature in her free and wild compositions,' wrote Chatham in his usual high-flown style, 'and I tell myself, as we go, that the *general mother* is not ashamed of her child.' Even when William took part in amateur theatricals, a very fashionable diversion for the young gentlemen and noblemen of his day, he wrote the play himself and made sure that it had a suitably political theme which would please his father. It was a tragedy in five acts, written in blank verse when he was only thirteen, and entitled *Laurentius King of Clarinium*. Laurentius having temporarily disappeared, his enemies seek to establish a Regency; but one faithful politician, with whom William seems to have identified himself, remains faithful to his absent master and is duly rewarded when the king returns and scatters his enemies. Curiously enough an almost exactly similar drama was to take place in 1788-9, when George III recovered from a bout of mental illness to find that he owed the preservation of his regal powers to his minister William Pitt, who had prevented the King's enemies from establishing a Regency.

But William's boyhood, though it might seem to look forward to his own political future, was really centred on the political past of his father. Chatham always tried to spend some time each day with his children, instructing them and reading to them from the Bible; and as his own political career disintegrated, from the late 1760s onwards, such sessions became more possible and also more necessary to the ageing statesman who conducted them. William was frequently given individual attention or was kept on, after his brothers and sisters had been dismissed, in order that his father might train him in the ways of the House of Commons and pass on to him the increasingly bitter fruits of his own political experience. The boy had to recite passages of Shakespeare and Milton and he also had to read aloud in English from books in other languages, translating as he went along in order to develop his fluency and his control over words. There were even those who later claimed that they had seen him placed upon a mounting-block in the garden and made to address the trees as though they were the members of the House of Commons. 'When I was a lad,' said Pitt later in life, 'my father used every evening to make me translate freely, before him and the rest of the family, those portions of Livy, Virgil, &c., which I had read in the morning with my tutor, Mr Wilson.' There were periods of liberation as well: the boy was sent on seaside holidays and was encouraged to ride as much as possible in the hope that the exercise would benefit his extremely delicate health. But even his medical treatment was a heritage from his father. The real cause of his constant illnesses, which was almost certainly a series of infections of the nose and throat, was ignored and it was assumed instead that he had inherited his father's gout. Dr Addington prescribed regular drinking of port wine, a medicine which was already doing more harm than good to Pitt the father and was eventually to hasten the death of Pitt the son. The nose and throat trouble, together with the fevers and other illnesses it brought with it, cleared up when William was in his teens; but the need for the prescribed medicine continued to be felt. In a sense it was indeed a remedy of sorts for an inherited weakness, but the weakness was not gout. It was something less easily definable and well beyond the diagnostic skills of Dr Addington: a kind of

OPPOSITE Lady Chatham's brother, George Grenville, whose interest in finance and administration was inherited by the younger Pitt.

Rt Hon: Geo: Grenville

detachment, a lofty isolation of oneself from the common run of humanity. In the father it produced, in spite of the dedicated love and companionship of Lady Chatham, periods of depression and self-doubt which bordered on madness. The son was to be less fortunate, finding no love and little companionship and turning instead to a lonely self-discipline which was made more bearable, but in the end more destructive, by steadily increasing doses of port wine.

However dominant Chatham may have been in the boy's life, passing on to him his torments and his vision, there were other factors as well. William's mother was as remarkable as his father and he remained in awe of her right up to the moment of her death, which took place only three years before his own. She had all the down-to-earth practicality of the Grenville family and she used it in order to create a framework within which the stormy and self-dramatising genius of her husband could have its fullest scope. And when that genius had conquered an empire it was a Grenville, Lady Chatham's brother George, who had taken up the humdrum task of governing it. That same Stamp Act which Chatham had expected to provoke suitably patriotic feelings in his seven-year-old son had been the work of George Grenville, busily reading the colonial dispatches and plodding through the tedious calculations and detailed schedules which the haughty impatience of his brother-in-law waved aside. Young William was brought up to respect the rhetoric rather than the arithmetic, to share his father's supreme contempt for those who thought that politics was a matter of sums and statistics. Lady Chatham herself never lost her admiration for her husband's transcendent genius: towards the end of her life, when her son's appetite for statistical detail had already done much to rescue the political and administrative system which Chatham's heady politics had put into jeopardy, she still declared unhesitatingly that her husband had been far cleverer than her son could ever be. Yet it remained true that the Grenville ability to handle facts and figures, which William had inherited from his mother along with her looks and much of her temperament, was to be an essential ingredient in his future success. In an age of economic expansion and government intervention, an age in which the new complexities of society could only be regulated with the help of bureaucrats and statisticians, it was as well that he was able to temper the sweeping visions of a Pitt with the detailed calculations of a Grenville.

Pembroke College, Cambridge. The rooms occupied by William Pitt are on the left of the first floor.

On 8 October 1773 William arrived at Pembroke College Cambridge, an unhealthy looking child of fourteen and a half who was accompanied by his tutor and was, so his father assured the college authorities, 'too young for the irregularities of a man'. Before he had had a chance to prove or disprove this assertion the boy fell dangerously ill, spending most of his first term confined to his rooms and too weak either to take up his studies or to return home. He finally managed to get home at the end of the year, taking four days over the journey because of his weakened condition, and he did not return to the University until the following summer. He spent the long vacation there but went back home in October, just as his fellow undergraduates were coming up, because his parents did not want to risk his spending another winter away from home. The same pattern was followed next year: five months in Cambridge, from May to September 1775, and then home again for the winter. Only in 1776, when he was seventeen, did he begin to keep regular terms and live something approaching the normal

OVERLEAF The collapse of the Earl of Chatham in the House of Lords, by Copley.

life of a Cambridge undergraduate. The shadow of his father was beginning to lift: the decade which had begun in July 1766, when Chatham first looked for patriotic feelings and sage reflections from his younger son, was at last coming to an end. The physical weakness which had kept William at home for so long, a willing captive of Chatham's mesmeric spell, seemed now to be cured and he became daily more robust and more self-sufficient. Cambridge reinforced and extended the teachings of his father and of his tutors, but it also offered new delights. He was particularly fascinated by the writings of Sir Isaac Newton, the seventeenth-century mathematician and physicist whose lucid explanation of the physical universe seemed to many eighteenth-century thinkers to show that all human problems, moral as well as practical, could be solved by means of a rational and mathematical approach. Young William Pitt did not perhaps go that far – nobody who had sat at Chatham's feet for ten years could believe that human beings were rational and perfectible creatures – but at least he valued 'the habit of close attention and patient investigation' which he found the study of Newtonian physics required.

When Chatham died, in May 1778, it was William who felt the loss and bore the burden: both his brothers were abroad on active service and so it fell to him to walk as chief mourner in the magnificent procession which bore his father's remains to a state funeral in Westminster Abbey. The last public appearance of Pitt the elder was thus the first public appearance of Pitt the younger. Once he had seen his father buried he would return to Cambridge, to continue those studies which were developing the Grenville in him as well as the Pitt and were opening up worlds undreamed of in his father's philosophy; but in the meantime there was the Pitt political heritage to be considered.

2

THE YOUNG PATRIOT

As soon as he got back from his father's funeral William sat down to write to his mother about it, assuring her that 'it had everything essential to the great object, the attendance being most respectable and the crowd of interested spectators immense'. Even in their private griefs the Pitts did not forget that they were public figures whose 'great object' must be to command attention and win support. The interested spectators were no doubt duly impressed, not merely by the melancholy magnificence of the occasion but also by the lonely distinction of the nineteen-year-old youth who walked at the head of all the famous politicians who had gathered to do his father honour. Here surely was a future leader, an heir who would step effortlessly and confidently into the heritage bequeathed to him by the great Chatham. Chatham himself might have become in his old age a slightly tarnished Patriot, but his son would rekindle the flame and re-animate the cause his father had once served. His youthful idealism and integrity, as well as his illustrious name, would enable him to remain true to the inheritance he was about to claim.

In fact there were many difficulties, both about the claiming and about the remaining true. The opposition politicians who came together at Westminster Abbey that day, turning the funeral by their very presence into something like a demonstration against the King and his ministers, were far too concerned with their own ambitions to promote the career of the adolescent chief mourner, however much they might mingle flattery with their condolences. Chatham had been out of the House of Commons for the past twelve years and out of active political life for nearly seven, with the result that other men had hastened to step into his shoes without waiting for his son to make his appearance. Lord Shelburne, an avowed disciple of Chatham who was generally regarded as his political heir, had already built up a small but formidable following in the House of Commons as well as among his fellow peers. The Marquis of Rockingham, the acknowledged successor of Newcastle as leader of the old Whig party, cut a fine figure at the funeral and was suitably affable both to Shelburne and to the young Mr Pitt; but in private he and most of his party regarded Shelburne as devious and Pitt – or at any rate the reformist aspirations which he seemed to have inherited – as deluded. The Rockingham Whigs had been for the past eight years the hard core of the opposition to Lord North, the minister who had taken over from Grafton in 1770 the dis-

PREVIOUS PAGE William Pitt as a young man.

The monument to William Pitt, Earl of Chatham, in the north transept of Westminster Abbey.

Three of the most powerful men in the Commons when Pitt entered politics were Lord Shelburne (left) a disciple of his father; the Marquis of Rockingham (centre) leader of the Whigs (painted with his secretary Edmund Burke); and Lord North (right) who had been leader of the administration since 1770.

credited remnants of the Chatham administration. During those eight years two harsh realities had become apparent: firstly that the quarrel with the American colonists could only be resolved by force and secondly that the only practicable alternative to corrupt party government by the Whigs was corrupt party government by – or on behalf of – the King. For Chatham and the Patriots these truths were too unpalatable to be recognised, since between them they destroyed the whole Patriot position; but for North they had provided the basis of a skilful and very successful political strategy. The Rockinghams hated him because he had turned their own weapons against them, using Whig techniques to buttress a 'King's Friend' ministry, while the Patriots hated him because he had prostituted and defiled their ideals, turning their reformist crusade against Whiggery into a reactionary crusade against the American colonists and against the liberties which those colonists were now defending.

This triangle of forces posed some tricky problems for the

young William Pitt, especially as there were still two years to go before he would be old enough to enter the House of Commons. He had to prepare himself for entry into the triangle without knowing how the forces it represented were going to shift or whereabouts his own entry would in the end prove most advantageous. Many of the independent country gentlemen who had once supported his father were now supporting Lord North: for them Patriot politics consisted in saving the King from the Whigs and the country from the American rebels. Others had turned to Rockingham, feeling that governmental tyranny had reached such proportions that only the practical experience and massive resources of the old Whig party could resist it. A few – very few – shared Shelburne's vision of a forward-looking and reformist Patriotism which refused to compromise either with North or with the Whigs. In many ways this was the line which might have been expected to attract William the most. It avoided the need for an ugly choice between Whigs and 'King's Friends' and it also provided scope for the Grenville

OVERLEAF Cambridge in the late eighteenth century, from a drawing by J. Ireland.

in him as well as the Pitt: several of Shelburne's friends and advisers were intellectuals of one kind or another, men who believed that the precise and calculating approach of Newtonian physics could with profit be applied to economic and political affairs. Unfortunately, however, radicals of this kind did not appeal to the independents whom Chatham had once led – any more than they would have appealed to Chatham himself if he had still been alive. Then, of course, there was the unwelcome presence of Shelburne himself, who was only just over forty and might well have many years of active political life ahead of him. If Pitt joined either Rockingham or North he would at least have the consolation and distinction of being the only Pittite in the party, whereas in Shelburne's group he would be only an heir to an heir, the political lieutenant of his father's lieutenant.

For two years young Mr Pitt watched and waited. He had taken his degree in Cambridge in 1776 at the age of seventeen, availing himself of the provision which allowed sons of noblemen to dispense with the commonplace and demeaning business of actually sitting an examination, and he was now

ABOVE The courtyard of Lincoln's Inn where Pitt completed his education.

OPPOSITE The Court of Chancery in Lincoln's Inn Hall.

ABOVE St James's and Pall Mall where Pitt's club, Goostree's, was a new rival to Boodle's and Brooks's in St James's Street (opposite).

rounding off his studies at the University and getting ready to read law at Lincoln's Inn in London. The rest of 1778 and most of 1779 were spent at his College and then, early in 1780, he moved to Lincoln's Inn, where his chambers cost him the 'frightful sum' of eleven hundred pounds. His social life, however, was already taking him far beyond the confines of College rooms or lawyers' chambers. Rather surprisingly, this stiff and somewhat solemn young man was developing, now that his father was dead, a taste for the fashionable social round and an ability to shine in it. There were frequent parties and drinking bouts and also a certain amount of gambling, although this was a pastime upon which he very soon turned his back. He even took a leading part in the formation of a new London club – Goostree's, in Pall Mall – to rival the splendours of such places as Boodle's and Brooks's, where the rich and powerful young men of England amused themselves during the London season. He was particularly at home in that most English of all social rituals, the exclusively male conversation over port and dessert at the end of a dinner party. There is a famous story of his demolishing the self-opinionated pomposity of Edward Gibbon on such an occasion so effectively that the infuriated historian got up and left the party. But there were also parties which Pitt himself desperately wanted to leave early. 'I was heartily tired of my domino before it was over', he confessed to his mother after attending a masked ball in April 1780. When it came to flirting with women rather than arguing with men he was a great deal less confident. And in a society which regarded a taste for fornication as a necessary proof of virility, this particular form of shyness did his reputation no good. It was not long before his political opponents were sneering at his alleged impotence.

Apart from this particular omission there were few ways in which he failed to prepare himself for acceptance into the political world. He talked and lived politics, not only in London but also in Cambridge, where his links with the Duke of

WAY of the WORLD
Who the Dupe

Rutland and other magnates encouraged him to think that he might one day hope to represent the University in the House of Commons. Nor was Rutland the only one of his friends to control boroughs and wield political influence. William Lowther, whom Pitt had known and liked since 1776, was the cousin of one of the richest and most ruthless political bosses in the northern counties of England. Others of his friends stood for different values and were reminders of his father's vaunted independence rather than of Whig borough-mongering. There was John Pratt, whose father Lord Camden was an old crony of Chatham and had played a notoriously vigorous part, as Lord Chief Justice, in the political upheavals of the 1760s. There was also Lord Euston, whose father the Duke of Grafton had followed with enthusiasm Chatham's non-party and anti-party line, only to find himself abandoned in 1768 and forced to take over the ministry which his chief had disowned. In fact Pitt's immediate social circle posed the same difficulties as the more distant political triangle upon which his eyes were fixed. How was he to choose between the comforting power of the great Whig families and the dangerous enthusiasm of the Patriot idealists?

The determining factor was money. 'Open' seats, seats in constituencies with electorates too large to be controlled by any one patron, were very prestigious but also very expensive to contest. Genuine independence in the House of Commons was a luxury limited to a few lucky men who were either rich enough to take on a large urban constituency or sufficiently well established in their county to be elected by their respectful neighbours with little or no opposition. And Chatham, however successful he might have been in using his 'Great Commoner' pose as a stepping-stone to ennoblement, had not been able to strike roots in his locality and turn his family into an accepted county dynasty within one generation. Nor had he left much money: he had lived like a lord even before he became one and during the final years of his life his expenditure had been colossal. He had died in debt and Parliament had had to pay off his creditors and had also voted an annuity of £4,000 a year for his dependants. In spite of these generous provisions there was little enough left for William when all the mortgages and other encumbrances of the estate had been sorted out. Pitt the elder had bequeathed to Pitt the younger the need, but not the means, to be politically independent.

The one constituency which seemed to offer all that the young

Pitt was more at home in the all-male society of a club (opposite above) than in the gay frivolity of a theatre lobby (below).

man required was the University of Cambridge. He told his mother in July 1779 that he had 'very good reason' to think that he might be elected for it – 'a seat of all others the most desirable, as being free from expense, perfectly independent, and I think in every respect extremely honourable'. When he heard that Parliament was dissolved and a General Election ordered, in September 1780, he hurried immediately to Cambridge and promoted his candidacy as energetically as he could. His hopes were bitterly disappointed – he came bottom of the poll and received less than a sixth of the votes cast – and he went on to Cheveley, the country house of his friend the Duke of Rutland, for consolation. Within a few weeks Rutland was able to produce consolation of a material kind. He spoke to Sir James Lowther, who had a seat to spare since his cousin William, Pitt's friend, had been put up for two Lowther-controlled boroughs and had been returned for both. The one he did not need, Appleby in Westmorland, was offered to Pitt on condition that he should give it up 'if ever our lines of conduct should become opposite'. It was a comparatively generous offer, as Lowther was a notoriously strict political master who usually made his followers in the Commons commit themselves in advance to his own line. If he did not do so on this occasion it was presumably because of his respect for the young Mr Pitt and for the name he bore. 'Judging from my father's principles,' William told his mother, 'he concludes that mine would be agreeable to his own.' Some months earlier, before the Cambridge fiasco, Lord Temple's offer of a seat had been refused because it would have compromised the proud Pitt tradition of independence – even though Temple was a cousin and himself subscribed to that tradition. Now it was too late for such scruples. Even an eighteenth-century General Election had to end eventually, protracted though it was as candidates unsuccessful in one constituency intrigued for support in another. And this one was coming to an end by late November, when the offer of the seat at Appleby was made. If that offer was refused there might not be another chance and Pitt might find himself out of Parliament for the next seven years.

Accordingly he made the best of a bad job and accepted the seat, entering the House of Commons in January 1781 when it reassembled at the end of the Christmas recess. After all, his father had done much the same thing: in 1747 and again in 1754 he had been returned for boroughs which were completely in the pocket of the Duke of Newcastle and which he did not

MR. MANGLES respectfully requests those of his worthy Friends, who may be disposed to celebrate his return to Parliament by their own fire sides as on the last occasion to send the inclosed Dinner Ticket, on or before THURSDAY the 2d of APRIL next, to his Agent MR. G. S. SMALLPEICE who will in exchange for such Ticket, give the Bearer thereof an Order for

TWELVE POUNDS OF BEEF,
ONE GALLON OF STRONG BEER,
TWO QUARTERN LOAVES,
THREE POUNDS AND A HALF OF FLOUR,
TWO POUNDS OF SUET,
TWO POUNDS OF RAISINS,
ONE POUND OF CURRANTS,
AND
TWO BOTTLES OF WINE, (PORT OR SHERRY).

MR. MANGLES also begs respectfully to inform those Friends who may not feel disposed to dine in public, and may not wish themselves to exchange the Dinner Ticket, that the same is transferrable to any of their Neighbors.

An Answer is respectfully requested to be sent to MR. G. S. SMALLPEICE, on or before THURSDAY the 2nd of APRIL next.

Russells, Printers, Guildford.

Free meals were a popular form of bribery in eighteenth-century elections.

even have to visit, any more than his son now bothered to go up to Appleby and show himself to the 250 burghers of that town who dutifully elected him as their member. Pitt the father had not allowed his obligations to one particular borough-monger to prevent him from attacking the borough-mongering structure as a whole and erecting his first 'Patriot' ministry as a challenge to it. In similar fashion it should be possible for Pitt the son to be a Patriot in spite of his connections with Lowther.

In fact the son's achievement was to be even more spectacular than that of the father. In March 1784, little more than three years after his first entry into this Parliament, he was himself to advise the King to dissolve it, even though it had run for less than four out of the seven years which eighteenth-century

Parliaments were normally expected to last. He was to be by this time not merely the King's first minister but his Patriot saviour, royally chosen to rescue the monarchy from the violence of the Rockingham Whigs, from the duplicity of Lord North and from the caution and cowardice of the Earl of Shelburne. And he was to be swept back to power on the shoulders of a new Parliament which reflected the electorate's disgust at the party bosses – a disgust already expressed in an unprecedented chorus of loyal addresses to the King even before the dissolution. Cambridge University itself, the constituency which had sent Pitt scurrying into the arms of Sir James Lowther in 1781, was to return him proudly at the head of the poll in 1784 and keep him there for the rest of his life. Pitt the elder had had to spend more than twenty years moving from one pocket borough to another before he had finally found a measure of independence as member for Bath; but Pitt the younger was to require only three years of skilful political manoeuvring in order to make himself eligible for a lifetime's occupancy of 'a seat of all others the most desirable' and to establish himself as the greatest of all the Patriots, a minister independent of all existing parties and owing allegiance only to his King and to his country.

The first steps towards this triumphant conclusion were taken within a few weeks of his entering Parliament. At the end of February 1781 a group of opposition members called on him by name to make a contribution to the debate, which was on a motion put up by the Rockingham Whigs to reduce the number of offices that the ministry had at its disposal to buy up members of Parliament. It was extremely unusual for a maiden speech to be made in this way: normally the new member was only expected to deliver a set speech prepared in advance and bearing little relation to the cut and thrust of debate. Pitt acquitted himself extraordinarily well, squashing the arguments of the previous speaker and prompting even the experienced Lord North to remark that it was the best maiden speech he had ever heard. Edmund Burke, who was spokesman for the Rockingham party in this matter of pruning government offices, declared in an often-quoted phrase that young William was not merely a chip off the old block but the old block itself. Others commented that if he had only had a few wrinkles in his face they would have thought they were listening to Chatham himself. When he next rose to speak, at the end of May, 'the House received him with all that silent attention which his former display of abilities, and the recollection of his illustrious descent, could not fail to command'.

At first it seemed as though his main aim was to use the display of abilities in order to underline the illustrious descent. He was particularly anxious to defend his father's views on the American question and he was furious when Richard Rigby and William Adam, two of North's supporters, suggested that Chatham was partly responsible for the war against the colonists since he had insisted on England's right to tax them. William replied by trotting out the tired old Chathamite distinction between the illegality of internal taxes, raised for purposes of revenue, and the legality of external taxes levied for the regulation of commerce. In fact it had been Chatham's own Chancellor of the Exchequer, Charles Townshend, who had brought the American revolution a stage nearer in 1767 by trying to exploit this unreal and legalistic distinction. But nobody in the House of Commons in 1781 dared to point this out to the angry young man as he thundered on about North's 'accursed, wicked, barbarous, cruel, unnatural, unjust and diabolical war'.

By the time the next session of Parliament opened, on 27 November, there was another and far more damning adjective to be added to this list. News had just arrived of Cornwallis's surrender to the American and French forces at Yorktown. The backbenchers might forgive North for waging a war that was unnatural and unjust, but they would not stomach for long a war that was now shown to be irredeemably unsuccessful. North himself recognised this in private, even though in public he put a brave front on things, drafting a confident speech for the King to deliver to Parliament and an equally confident Address of Thanks for the Commons to return to the King. Pitt immediately took the lead in opposing this Address, but at first he got comparatively little support. Only fifty-four members followed him into the opposition lobby on 28 November but he persisted in his campaign and the support for it grew steadily. Rockingham and Shelburne watched excitedly from the House of Lords as the final assault on North gathered momentum in the other House; but all their confidence and all their assured anticipation of high office could not conceal the fact that it was an independent young man of twenty-two, a self-proclaimed Patriot rather than a party man, who was really making the running. Pitt spoke at least seven times more during those crucial weeks, always on the same theme of the bad and bungled war. On 7 February 1782, when he acted as Teller for the Noes on a motion charging the ministry with incompetence, he secured 217 votes and reduced North's majority to nineteen. When the end came on 15 March, with the carrying of a motion of censure on the administration, he contrived to be in at the kill and to give it a flourish of his own. He made one of the concluding speeches in favour of the motion and he violently attacked North's rumoured intention of staying in power in order to make some sort of coalition with his victorious opponents. 'Was this a work fit to be entrusted to the noble lord,' asked Pitt scathingly, 'and to be settled by him in his closet? The administration of the noble lord in the blue ribbon has been an administration of influence and intrigue.'

But however much the young Patriot might declaim against influence and intrigue, against the piecemeal construction of administrations by means of bargains between individuals and coalitions between parties, the hard political fact remained that there was no other way of governing the country. There was not going to be a new dawn of Patriotism in 1782, any more than there had been sixteen years earlier when Chatham had embarked on his disastrous flight of idealism. Most men were in politics for what they could get out of it, for offices or peerages or pensions or perquisites; and the only thing that was new about the Rockingham Whigs was their determination to change the way in which such things were bestowed, in order that the King should never again be able to exclude them from office as he had done for the past sixteen years. They devoted the minimum of time to intrigue, making a hurried coalition with Shelburne and taking office at the end of March, and then they turned to the problem of influence. They introduced measures for the reform of government offices, those same measures that Pitt had supported in his maiden speech a year earlier, but their real aim was to reduce the powers and patronage of the King rather than to reform the comfortable and lucrative business of party politics. When Pitt proposed reform in a wider sense at the beginning of May, seeking to air schemes for electoral reform which the Rockinghams themselves had appeared to support while in opposition, he got a very cool reception from the new administration. Burke, busy with his plans to abolish offices which benefited the King and preserve offices which benefited the Whigs, 'attacked William Pitt in a scream of passion and swore that Parliament was and always had been precisely what it ought to be and that all people who thought of reforming it wanted to overturn the Constitution'.

On the issue of reform, as on the issue of America, Pitt took care to pose as 'the old block itself' and to give that same impression of filial devotion and paternal resurrection which had already been such a help to him. Referring to his father somewhat portentously as 'a certain person', he delivered a solemn warning as to what might happen if Chatham's prophetic advice on this matter were ignored:

> He personally knew that it was the opinion of that person that without recurring to first principles in this respect and establishing a more solid and equal representation of the people, by which the proper constitutional connection could be revived, this nation, with the best capacities for grandeur and happiness of any on the face of the earth, must be confounded with the mass of those whose liberties were lost in the corruption of the people.

Pitt's motion, which was cast in the vaguest terms in order to gain the widest possible measure of support, was only lost by twenty votes; but when the reformers went on to make specific proposals the hostility of the Rockinghams became more obvious. It was a motion for shorter Parliaments that evoked Burke's notorious 'scream of passion' and it was a Bill for the prevention of bribery at elections that drew down on Pitt the even more unexpected opposition of Charles Fox, supposedly the most progressive of the Rockinghams and now Foreign Secretary in the new administration. 'Why should we endeavour to circumscribe,' asked Fox indignantly, 'the very few privileges of the electors of Great Britain?' The idea that the right to be bribed was an essential part of English liberty was not made explicit, but it was there all the same. 'A certain person' might have felt that reform was necessary in the defence of freedom, but that person's son would have some difficulty in distinguishing the defenders of freedom from the defenders of privilege.

Within a matter of weeks the situation had changed dramatically and it was not the liberties of England but the monarchy of England that needed Patriot defence. Rockingham died suddenly on 2 July 1782 and the tensions which had long existed within his administration came into the open. Shelburne, who as Home Secretary had thought (and sometimes even spoken) of the ministry as his own, prepared to assume control with the approval of the King: George III knew well enough that if North would not or could not serve him then Shelburne, the

The Duke of Portland, after Reynolds.

political heir of Chathamism and of Patriotism, was his best defence against the Whigs. The Whigs for their part denied Shelburne's right to take over and insisted instead that the King must accept the Duke of Portland, their chosen nominee, as Rockingham's successor. Portland was not a very able man – 'it is not merely that a few great families claim the hereditary and exclusive right of giving us a head,' wrote Horace Walpole tartly, 'but they will insist upon selecting a head without a tongue' – and it was clear that Fox would be the real prime minister. George III and Shelburne refused to give way and so three days after Rockingham's death Fox resigned, followed by Burke and by one or two others. The main body of the Rockingham Whigs stayed in, but there were serious gaps in the ministry which would have to be plugged if the King's government were to be carried on.

Here at last was a situation in which the application of Chatham's principles led not to doubts and difficulties but to decision. His ideas on America and even on reform might have been overtaken by events, but his attitude to party leaders who tried to bully their way into power was still highly relevant. Fox might be the darling of the radicals, the defender of American liberties and even something of a reformer when it suited him, but in this instance he was the exponent of old Whiggism at its worst – 'the wretch who draws the great families at his heels', as Chatham had once said of Newcastle. And the determination to serve only under Portland and not under Shelburne was an example of putting 'men before measures', one of the cardinal sins according to the Chathamite political morality. Patriot politics meant finding a cause you could serve, a programme you could believe in, rather than a clique of friends you happened to like. As Pitt was quick to point out in a debate on the ministerial changes, those who had resigned could point to nothing in Shelburne's policies which they opposed outright. It was the man, not his measures, that they disliked. In such a crisis it seemed right and proper that the young Patriot should rally to the minister of the King's choice. While in public Shelburne appealed to Chatham's memory, recalling that 'that noble earl always declared that the country ought not to be governed by any oligarchical party or family connection', in private he appealed to Chatham's son, offering him the post of Chancellor of the Exchequer. This had just been vacated by Lord John Cavendish, political head of one of the most powerful of the 'great families', who had been drawn into resignation at Fox's heels.

Charles James Fox, the most radical and talented of Pitt's opponents.

The offer did not take Pitt by surprise. As soon as he had heard of Rockingham's death he had concluded that it would result in a reshuffled cabinet 'in which I *may*, and probably *ought*, to take a part'. Friendly observers might see his appointment as a Patriot response to a Whig challenge, but there was room also for a more hostile interpretation according to which his sudden elevation to high office was the climax of a deep-laid plot to oust the Rockinghams, a plot which had its origins in the bad feeling which the King had from the beginning fostered between the two wings of his administration. When Parliament met again on 5 December the new Chancellor of the Exchequer got a hostile reception and there was much derisive comment on his extreme youth. His father had been similarly taunted more than forty years before and had crushed his enemies with the famous retort: 'The atrocious crime of being a young man . . . I shall neither attempt to palliate or deny.' William found it difficult to rise to such sublime heights of contempt. He rounded petulantly on his tormentors, telling them that 'the present was a moment for seriousness and not for mirth' and deploring the fact that his youth 'had been made the subject for animadversion'. As the session wore on he became more peevish and less controlled. In February 1783 he made himself look rather silly by attacking George Johnstone in the most violent terms for seconding a motion which he had not seconded at all. A few days later he allowed himself some cheap sarcasm about Sheridan's links with the theatre, drawing down on himself a devastating retort from the playwright as a result.

These lapses were understandable, for Pitt was under tremendous pressure during the winter of 1782-3. In theory he was simply the Chancellor of the Exchequer, his responsibilities limited to matters of finance and administration, but in fact he was Shelburne's only effective spokesman in the House of Commons and thus had to face the whole force of the opposition's attack. In reality there were two attacks: Lord North and his followers suspected that Shelburne was being too soft on the American colonists and was about to conclude a peace which would throw away all that the war had been fought for, while the Whigs feared that the peace would not be soft enough and would alienate those forces in America which the Rockingham administration had sought to conciliate. Pitt was exasperated almost beyond endurance by the constant attempts to trap him into revealing the details of the negotiations which were in progress. 'Did any member ever hear,' he demanded furiously, 'of ministers rising up in their places and proclaiming to the House the secrets of a treaty still pending?' One thing he did give away: he announced in quite explicit terms that the recognition of American independence was unconditional and would not be revoked even if the negotiations for peace broke down. This statement angered the King, who still seemed to think that his rebellious subjects across the Atlantic could be put down by force if they refused to agree to terms. But Pitt would not retract and the Shelburne ministry stood committed to an American policy more liberal than George III's and possibly more liberal than that of Shelburne himself, whose position, on this as on so many other matters, was hard to determine. Pitt might seem to be a lightweight in politics, a young man lacking both experience and connections, but he was already capable of getting his own way on vital policy decisions.

The reason for his obstinacy became clear half way through February, when the ministry submitted the terms of the American peace treaty to Parliament and suffered a series of defeats. Amid mounting speculation, rumours of resignations and coalitions and wholesale change, William Pitt worked behind the scenes to restore stability to British politics. More than a decade ago his father had told Rockingham that 'the *whole* alone can save the *whole* against the desperate designs of the Court'; and in Pitt's judgment this was still true. North and his followers, with their vindictive determination to justify their 'unjust and diabolical war', still stood for the same desperate designs that they urged upon their King in the 1770s. If the King still believed them, still clung to the delusions of imperial power that they had fed him, then he must be saved from himself. Pitt saw himself in the same position that his father had occupied, recalling the King on the one hand and the politicians on the other to their true duty. In July 1782 he had helped to teach the Rockinghams that they could not push their way into power by unconstitutional means; six months later he had taught the King that he could not ignore the realities of the American situation. Now he would put the two halves of his policy together and persuade the King to accept a broadly based administration in which all right-minded politicians, Rockingham Whigs and Shelburne Whigs alike, could come together to extinguish once and for all the malign influence of Lord North. Ever since boyhood William Pitt had regarded government by North as the ultimate political evil: incompetent, corrupt, tyrannous and wrong-headed. Differences between honourable men, Whigs or Patriots or whatever, might come and go, but their refusal to work with North would – or at any rate should – go on for ever.

It did not. North's position had been getting stronger ever since Christmas, when the disagreements over American independence had begun to split the Shelburne ministry. However much Pitt might want his chief to side with the Whigs against North, there were those who wanted a Shelburne–North alliance against the Whigs. Shelburne tried for it, but too late. His overtures to North only divided his own following still more. Henry Dundas, a junior minister in the Shelburne ministry, tried to frighten North by suggesting that there were now four forces in politics and not three: if North did not come to terms with Shelburne both of them might be crushed by the joint forces of Pitt and Fox. But North was too old a hand to be scared by that sort of thing and he began to move towards the alternative, the apparently unthinkable alternative, of a coalition with Fox. As well as being the effective leader of the Rockingham Whigs, North's implacable critics for many years, Fox was also a personal enemy of the fallen minister. He was the champion of the Americans, whom North had sought to subdue, and he was also the close friend of the Prince of Wales. This last was a consideration of some importance, for the associates of the King's heir seldom worked harmoniously with those of the King himself. Heirs to the throne tended to promise great things for the future and to gather around them young politicians who hoped for high office in the succeeding reign. Charles Fox was thirteen years older than the Prince and ten years older than Pitt, but he seemed to possess the secret of eternal youth just as surely as Pitt had the ability to appear middle-aged when scarcely out of his teens. The gap between Fox and North, like that between their respective royal patrons, was a generation gap as well as a political one.

And yet it was bridged. Fox and North somehow squared their conflicting views on America and agreed to oppose the French and Spanish aspects of the peace treaty, the allegedly unnecessary concessions to America's European allies, while skirting round the more controversial question of the concessions to the Americans themselves. Differences over parliamentary reform, like those on America, were put aside and each man agreed to respect the views of the other. In this way they isolated Shelburne, who resigned on 24 February 1783, and they also isolated the King, who was to spend the next six weeks looking in vain for a way to avoid a Fox–North administration. Perhaps most important of all, they isolated Pitt and everything he stood for. He had held to the idealist view of politics, the conviction that measures mattered more than men, and Fox and North had taught him a sharp lesson. They had shown him that naked ambition and a cynical contempt for principle could form a far more effective basis for united action than all the aspirations of the Patriots and all the schemes of the reformers. Pitt had shown more flexibility, more readiness to compromise, than either Shelburne or the King. He had not retreated into the realms of pure theory and intellectual speculation, as Shelburne seemed to have done, and he had opposed George III's rigid attitude to American independence. He had

OPPOSITE Pitt's coat of arms.

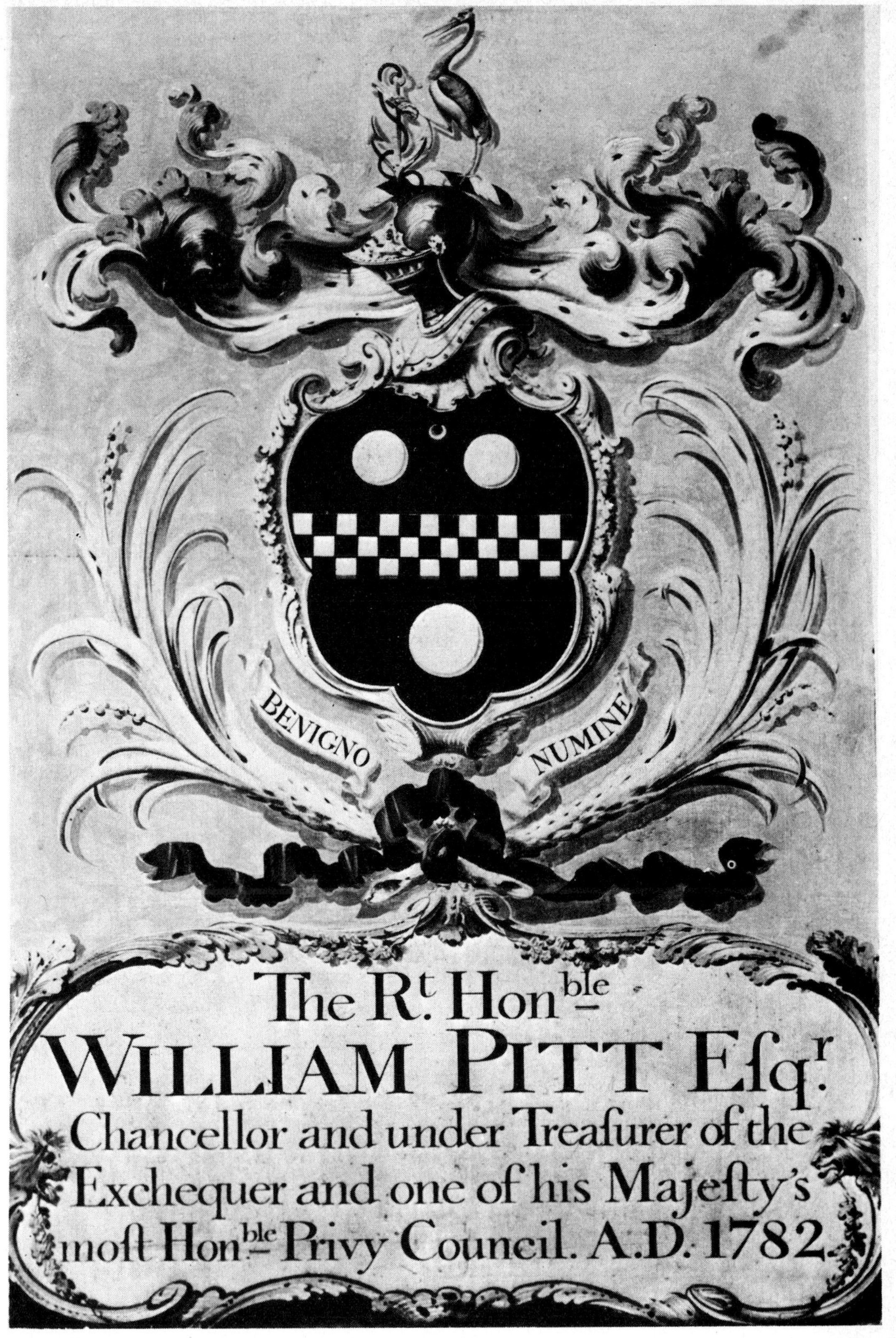
BENIGNO NUMINE
The Rt. Honble
WILLIAM PITT Esqr.
Chancellor and under Treasurer of the
Exchequer and one of his Majesty's
most Honble Privy Council. A.D. 1782

seen that the defeat in America meant not just the end of an empire but the end of the commercial policy that had held that empire together – something which his father would never have conceded, any more than he would have conceded American independence itself. While George III was the declared enemy of Whig party politics, Shelburne seemed to be the secret enemy of all existing politics, the advocate of sweeping but ill-defined change. Only Pitt seemed able to move in both worlds at once, the world of things as they actually were and the world of things as they might possibly be. It was for this reason that Fox and North, apparent enemies but in fact twin guardians of the comfortable world of patronage politics, had had to isolate him. It was for this reason that they must in the end destroy him or be destroyed by him.

Pitt did not give in easily. He repeated the charges he had made the previous summer, saying that the Rockinghams and their new allies were objecting to men rather than to measures, to Shelburne rather than to the treaty he had made. He defended the treaty valiantly, arguing that any faults it might have were the result of North's inability to make war rather than of Shelburne's inability to make peace. He held on to his office for five weeks after Shelburne's resignation, providing one of the few symbols of stability in a prolonged scene of political chaos. He consulted with the King on more than one occasion about the possibility of his forming an administration of his own. In company with seasoned political bosses like Richard Rigby and Henry Dundas he went through lists of the Commons to see whether he had any chance of getting a majority there. Once at the end of February and again at the end of March it seemed as though he had found a way of enlisting the necessary numbers, but on both occasions his hopes – and those of the King – were disappointed when he came to examine the political groupings more carefully. In the end he had to admit that with the House of Commons as it was there was no practicable alternative to a Fox–North administration. The young Patriot might have unparalleled insights into things as they ought to be, but the experienced borough-mongers of the Fox and North parties had an unbreakable control over things as they were. Pitt resigned his office on 31 March and then, after a few days of last-ditch resistance by the King, North and Fox came into office as co-equals, the one as Home Secretary and the other as Foreign Secretary, with the Duke of Portland as First Lord of the Treasury and titular head of the administration.

One more resource remained: the movement for parliamentary reform which was part of Pitt's inheritance from his father and which had already helped him to win support both inside and outside Parliament. There was no doubt that the Fox–North coalition was violently unpopular throughout the country. The House of Commons might therefore be brought to realise that if it did not reform itself it would soon share the discredit already being heaped upon the ministry it had endorsed. What an unreformed Parliament had done a reformed one might well undo. In a crucial and bitter debate in the middle of April Pitt admitted that in forming a ministry the King ought to listen to the voice of Parliament – 'it was at all times justifiable for it [the House of Commons] to interfere in the choice and continuance of His Majesty's ministers' – but he reserved his position on the associated issue of whether under existing electoral arrangements the voice of Parliament was necessarily the voice of the people. Early in May he brought in a motion to give definite shape to the general intentions of reform he had expressed a year earlier. He proposed that boroughs convicted of corruption should lose their right of representation and he also suggested that there should be additional members for the counties and for London. Fox – one of the relatively small number of Rockinghamites who had remained true to electoral reform even after Burke had produced the comforting idea of pruning offices instead – spoke and voted for the motion. So did some of his supporters: they

Brighton beach in the late eighteenth century, by Richard Earlom. Pitt took a holiday there in 1783.

could do so in complete security as North's men were determined not to let their newly acquired offices be jeopardised by any idealistic nonsense about reform. When it came to a division Pitt's supporters numbered 149, an increase of eight on the 141 who had voted for him the previous year; but his opponents had nearly doubled their numbers, from 161 to 293. Such was the result of moving from vague intentions to specific proposals. Such, too, was the result of proposing reform to a House of Commons which had just come down decisively on the side of those who stood to gain most from the perpetuation of the existing system.

It seemed that there was nothing more to be done. For the rest of the session Pitt dropped his single-minded pursuit of politics and spent an increasing amount of time at Goostree's Club and at Wimbledon, a village near London where his friend Wilberforce had a villa. He was relaxed and even exuberant – on one occasion his carousing was sufficiently wild to wake up the whole neighbourhood at Wimbledon – and this mood continued when he went on holiday after the parliamentary session ended in July. He spent some time at the newly fashionable seaside resort of Brighton and then he went down to Dorset for partridge-shooting by day and revelry by night at the house of his friend Henry Bankes. In September he and Wilberforce went to France with another friend, Edward James Eliot, who was later to marry Pitt's sister Harriot. Chatham had always inveighed against France as the home of tyranny and slavery, a country where wicked Bourbon kings kept their own people in misery in order to have enough revenue to make war on the liberties of the people of England; and so William was somewhat surprised to find that ordinary Frenchmen seemed to be quite comfortably off and that the French King was 'a clumsy strange figure in immense boots'. The three friends first spent some time in Rheims, which they found rather dull, and then went on to Paris and Versailles, where Pitt was taken up by fashionable society. It was all very amusing and rather flattering, a pleasant change from the harsh parliamentary conflicts in which he had been involved earlier in the year. Then, in the middle of October, a special messenger arrived in Paris to summon Pitt home. He was never again to take a holiday abroad and there was to be little enough leisure for him even in his own country. The overture to his career as a statesman was finished and the curtain was about to go up on the performance itself.

3

THE WORLD TURNED UPSIDE DOWN

IT WAS SAID that as the British forces marched out to surrender to the Americans at Yorktown the band played *The world turned upside down*, a strange and slightly macabre popular song with words that told of mice chasing cats and other reversals of the natural order. George Washington, the American general who received the capitulation, was certainly no enemy to the established order of society: he was one of the cats of this world and had no intention of encouraging the mice overmuch. Nevertheless the success of his campaigning had indeed turned many things upon their heads. The eighteenth-century world, the world which Chatham had helped to mould and which his son had been brought up to inherit, was crumbling fast. Within the four walls of the House of Commons, sitting where his father had sat and facing the men his father had faced, it was still possible for Pitt to feel that he was playing the game his father had played and that the rules had not changed very much. But wider perspectives gave clearer indications of change. Across the Channel in France he found himself surrounded by confident Frenchmen who no longer thought of England as the home of liberty but as the centre of corruption and incompetence. Twenty years earlier, when the first English visitors had arrived in Paris after the triumphant war his father had waged, France had received them with awe and admiration: fashionable Parisian society had been only too anxious to learn from the astonishing islanders whose parliamentary system and commercial drive had enabled them to conquer half the world. Now there was pity and patronage rather than reverence and respect. The name of Pitt – a name which had once been sufficient, according to Horace Walpole, to reduce any assembly of Frenchmen to terrified silence – was now of interest principally because it was associated with the movement for parliamentary reform. Frenchmen took it for granted that England's existing institutions were on the point of collapse and that her only chance of survival lay in submitting herself to reform before it was too late.

Little of this apocalyptic feeling had penetrated to the enclosed parliamentary world to which Pitt hurried back in the autumn of 1783. Earlier that year, after a speech in which he had defended Shelburne's peace treaty with the words 'Let us examine what is left', he had tried to make his countrymen realise that if they were going to salvage anything from the American disaster they must abandon the old system of protective tariffs and let the Americans trade freely with the

PREVIOUS PAGE The surrender of Lord Cornwallis at Yorktown in 1781.

OPPOSITE The Old East India Quay in the Port of London.

country that once ruled them. Fox and North, however, had thrown his free-trade schemes overboard and had gone back to the old protectionist ideas which his father had defended so fiercely and which had helped to bring about the American revolution. Having shorn the American settlement of the reciprocal trading concessions which might have made it work, the new ministers presented it to Parliament in November with scarcely any other alterations. Pitt asked scathingly how Fox and North could commend to the House in November the same treaty that they had attacked in February; but he did not press the question of free trade. However much he might himself realise that the world of Atlantic commerce had been turned upside down, he knew well enough that those whom he was addressing lived for the most part in the cosy and familiar world of commercial regulation and protected markets. Instead he challenged the ministry on the other great imperial issue of the time, the need to subject the chartered trading companies to proper governmental control. The East India Company was in a particularly absurd position, its original trading functions almost submerged by executive responsibilities which should clearly be supervised, if not actually exercised, by the King's administration in London. The new ministers were 'pledged and bound down,' Pitt insisted, 'to bring forward a well-weighed and wisely-digested system applicable to India'.

The ministers had in fact been weighing and digesting systems for India all through the summer; and within a week Pitt's challenge was taken up and proposals were tabled for an East India Board in London which would have sweeping powers over the Company's officials in India itself. In some ways the scheme looked forward to a new world, a new kind of imperialism within which professional administrators might eventually come to replace the self-seeking and sometimes highly irresponsible servants of commercial companies. But it also looked resolutely backward into the old world of patronage politics, for the Board was to be made up of Fox's and North's men and it was to be set up in such a way that its members could not be removed by subsequent administrations. Pitt immediately attacked the plan as 'absolute despotism', 'gross corruption' and 'one of the most bold and forward exertions of power that was ever adopted by ministers'. When the East India Bill came up for its first reading on 1 December he made more explicit charges against the ministers. 'Should they be driven from their places,' he warned, 'they would carry their influence with them into private life and it would be exerted against the Crown.'

That same day George III received a memorandum suggesting that the Crown should defend itself by bringing about the fall of the ministers before they had time to dig themselves in permanently with the help of East India patronage. One of the signatories of this document was Lord Temple, Pitt's cousin and political ally, who had already made it clear that in the present situation he thought that he and Pitt were the King's 'only resource'. While Pitt thundered away in the Commons, posing as the disinterested private citizen who wished only to defend the constitution, his cousin advised the King to use his influence in order to get the East India Bill defeated in the Lords, where the ministry's position was less secure than it was in the Commons. After some hesitation George III authorised secret negotiations with the Pitt–Temple group and there was some anxious consultation of parliamentary lists to see if the Fox–North control of the Commons could be broken by dissolving Parliament and holding a General Election. Richard Atkinson, leader of the resistance to Fox's Bill within the East India Company itself, told the King's political managers that the Company would provide funds to fight the election and that 'everything stands prepared for the blow if a certain person has the courage to strike it'. By 11 December the certain person's courage had been brought to the sticking-point: Temple was given authority to tell the House of Lords that any peer voting for the India Bill would be considered as the King's enemy, 'and if these words were not strong enough Earl Temple might use whatever words he might deem stronger and more to the purpose'. This statement of the King's intentions served its purpose and on 17 December the House of Lords threw out the Bill. George III then dismissed the Fox–North coalition and appointed twenty-four-year-old William Pitt as First Lord of the Treasury and Chancellor of the Exchequer.

At first sight it looked as though this was more like turning back the clock than turning the world upside down. The second William Pitt was to save the King from the fury and faction of the party leaders just as the first William Pitt had been supposed to do more than seventeen years before. But there were great differences between the situation in 1766 and that in 1783, differences so vital that they added up to a total transformation of the political scene. Chatham had come into office in 1766 because almost every party leader was crying out for him to do

ABOVE AND OPPOSITE
The exterior and interior of the East India House in Leadenhall.

so, because the existing political situation simply could not produce any other viable ministry; but his son came into power in the teeth of violent opposition from the two greatest political parties of the time, those of Fox and North, and a grudging and suspicious neutrality on the part of the third, that of the Earl of Shelburne. While Chatham had come to save the King from his own weaknesses, to end once and for all the malign influence of the royal favourite the Earl of Bute, Pitt was himself the favourite, the open and avowed instrument of royal influence. And if Chatham could be said to have betrayed the 'Great Commoner' tradition by going to the House of Lords in his moment of triumph, his son was now undermining that tradition in a far more sinister fashion by forcing upon a reluctant Commons a ministry begotten of a conspiracy in the House of Lords and made up almost entirely of members of

that House – Pitt himself was the only member of the Cabinet who sat in the Commons. Finally, there was a dramatic and extremely significant difference in the attitude of those who were called upon to join the ministry. In 1766 men had fallen over themselves to enlist under Chatham's banner, but now they turned their backs on his son. Service under Chatham had been seen as the ultimate prize, an honour which would add lustre to any political career; but service under his son in this desperate venture of December 1783 was seen as something which could jeopardise and possibly even terminate the most promising career.

Pitt was well aware of the difficulties and the differences. As he tried one independent politician after another, getting refusal after refusal, he soon realised that his chances of forming a 'Patriot' ministry in the tradition beloved of his father were

Richard, Lord Temple, in a painting by Hoare.

negligible. The Duke of Grafton, once such a devoted admirer of the Pitt family and its gallant defence of the monarchy against the party bosses, declined to serve: he had been let down once by Chatham and did not intend to be let down a second time by Chatham's son. Even the more faithful Chathamites like Lord Camden would have nothing to do with the new administration. In the end Pitt scraped together seven colleagues who would agree to form a ministry with him; but as well as being peers they were also for the most part either Tories, whom his father would have viewed with suspicion, or nonentities, whom his father would have viewed with contempt. Even Temple deserted him, resigning suddenly three days before Christmas for reasons which were not clear at the time and have not become any clearer since, in spite of much controversy among historians. Since he had been the person responsible for reporting the King's wishes to the House of Lords, the thing which Fox and North denounced as the most unconstitutional part of the whole December conspiracy, it might have been thought that he was a useful scapegoat whose voluntary departure into the wilderness should be welcomed rather than deplored; but Pitt bitterly regretted his going and even lost a night's sleep over it, a thing which for him was extremely unusual. Temple's departure underlined with stark clarity the loneliness of the new minister and the callousness with which the political world made ready to abandon him if his dramatic challenge to the Whig view of the constitution should prove unsuccessful.

But there were other differences between 1766 and 1783, differences which worked to Pitt's advantage. The greatest of these by far was the discredit of Parliament. If Chatham had been faced with the overwhelming hostility of the House of Commons he would have bowed to it, King or no King, because he and most of his supporters still believed that the voice of the Commons was the voice of those who elected it – the voice, that is to say, of the freeholders and freemen of England, Scotland and Wales. But now the electors of Britain were getting restless. They refused to stand in awe of an assembly which would not reform itself and which had failed so dismally to assert its right to rule America. When party leaders insisted – as Burke and others did on more than one occasion – that the duty of a member of Parliament was to his party rather than to his constituency, they merely widened the gulf between electors and elected and brought the House of Commons into even greater disrepute. Pitt was quick to make capital out of this disrepute: when his opponents called on him to resign because he did not have the support of the Commons, he retorted that he would do so if he had reason to believe that his successors would be acceptable to the people and not just to Parliament. When the House decided to put on one side a petition from Yorkshire for parliamentary reform he deplored the decision and declared that if 'the reform which the people had so much wished for' had been granted the result would have been a House of Commons which would have endorsed his entry into office instead of opposing it.

There was no justification for the suggestion that the people as a whole wanted parliamentary reform: the movement was a powerful one but it still represented only a minority of the electorate, which was itself only a tiny minority of the population. And if the reformers were discouraged by the conservatism of most electors, they were even more discouraged by the sheer apathy and disinterest of those who were not electors. Yet there were certain things that the people as a whole did feel strongly about; and the bullying of the King by the party leaders was undoubtedly one of them. Men of property and substance might be more convinced by Pitt's other argument, the insistence that he was defending chartered rights against those who wished to swallow them up, but humbler folk knew only that King George needed their support against the usurpations and impertinences of Charles Fox. While London crowds chanted menaces outside Fox's house and threatened to break his windows for him, caricaturists found a ready sale for prints identifying the Whig leader with Oliver Cromwell. All over the country freeholders and freemen met together to draw up loyal addresses to the King, assuring him of their support for him and for his youthful First Lord against the factious forces of Whiggery. There were well over two hundred of these addresses, far more than any other crisis of the century produced. In London, meanwhile, the excitement grew uglier and turned into open violence when a group of Whig thugs from Brooks's Club clashed with the crowds who were drawing Pitt's carriage home in triumph after he had been given the freedom of the City of London. The door of his coach was forced open and he had to take refuge in a neighbouring house in order to avoid being beaten up. The incident led to fresh troubles outside Fox's house and to accusations that the Whig leader had been responsible for the attack on his young rival.

Fox replied imperturbably that he had been in bed with his mistress at the time and knew nothing about it.

By the time this affray took place, on 29 February 1784, Pitt had succeeded in eroding his opponents' position in the House of Commons itself as well as in the country at large. When he first took office there was talk of an immediate dissolution, but he advised against this. Having been spurned by men like Grafton and deserted by a man like Temple, he had to show that his was a real administration with real policies, not just a narrowly based product of royal despotism. For his other great advantage, the other great difference which distinguished his first ministry from his father's last and showed how much the political world had changed, was the fact that he did have policies. The problem of India, the problem which his father had failed to solve in 1766, interested him for reasons that were practical as well as political. As a politician, as the son of Chatham, he had seen that Fox's India Bill provided ideal ground on which to challenge Whig patronage politics; but as an administrator, as the nephew of George Grenville, he saw also that India must be governed and not merely managed. While other opponents of Fox's Bill had concentrated almost entirely on the patronage issue, Pitt had gone into financial detail – boring his listeners and blunting his attack in the process. Now he proposed to do so again. If the backbenchers wanted the heroics they must be prepared to put up with the routine stuff as well. They must be made to realise that they now had a prime minister for whom the spectre of governmental inefficiency was even more alarming than that of governmental tyranny. They thought they were watching the rebirth of Chathamite Patriot politics, but in fact they were witnessing the birth of a cold new world of professional bureaucracy which Chatham would have viewed with horror.

Accordingly the Commons found, when they assembled again after the Christmas holidays, that Pitt was still there and that he refused to be ruffled either by rumours of imminent dissolution or by accusations of unconstitutional behaviour. They had no time, he insisted, for histrionics or idle gossip: 'Their first duty was to frame a system for the government of India.' Fox and North rocked with mirth, confident that they could prevent the House from framing anything, except perhaps votes of censure or proposals for the impeachment of this arrogant young man. Pitt had an India Bill ready and waiting, worked out in concert with the East India Company and

A contemporary engraving of George III's procession to Parliament.

politically unexceptionable: it gave the authorities in India itself a chance to govern efficiently and it provided for an India Board without the sweeping patronage powers and entrenched irremovability which Fox's Board would have had. His attempt to introduce it was blocked by the opposition, as was every other attempt at positive governmental action. Fox and North were determined to prove that they had the real power, that those who had the support of the Commons could frustrate and reduce to impotence ministers who had only the support of the King and of a rigged majority in the House of Lords. In the eyes of Pitt's opponents the British constitution implied parliamentary government, government by the consent of the House of Commons. Any other sort of government must surely be impossible and must therefore be shown to be impossible.

Pitt took his stand upon a different interpretation of the constitution, an interpretation which spoke of balance between King and Parliament – and of balance between the two Houses of Parliament themselves – rather than of the complete dominance of the Commons. When he was accused of being merely the tool of the King's prerogative powers he replied that 'Prerogative has been justly called a part of the rights of the people; and I am sure that it is a part of their rights which the people were never more disposed to defend, of which they were never more jealous, than at this hour'. As to the way in which he had been appointed, he staunchly and vehemently denied that it had been the result of secret intrigue or secret influence. It was he who had responded to the King's overtures, he insisted, and not the other way about: 'I came up no back stairs . . . I knew of no secret influence . . . I will never condescend to be the instrument of any secret advisers whatever'. The details of his secret negotiations early in December, which have only recently been revealed, make it clear that the charges against which he was defending himself were substantially true. His denials may not have been downright lies but they were certainly disingenuous. He had not stood by in aloof dignity until his sovereign had openly invited him to save the Crown; he had come into office as a result of intrigues which had been aimed deliberately at the destruction of a ministry which had a majority in the Commons.

The really remarkable thing about the crisis, the thing which Fox and North could hardly bring themselves to believe until it had actually happened, was that Pitt was able to win over the existing House of Commons to his side as well as the electors who would have to choose the next one. His tactics were simple: by behaving as though he had a perfect right to govern he placed the onus for the lack of government squarely on the opposition. Fox and North had a splendid time in January and February, passing votes of censure and striking constitutional attitudes amid scenes of wild enthusiasm. But eventually they had to face the simple and straightforward question: should they or should they not allow the King's government to continue? Were they prepared to take the ultimate step of withholding taxes and blocking the Mutiny Act, the legislation without which the army itself would become illegal? Extreme measures like these would undoubtedly lose them the support of the moderates, but failure to take them would displease the militants and would undermine their whole position on the constitutional issue. And so they hesitated, temporising and squirming in their attempts to challenge the King's minister without defying the King's government. 'It is pretty singular,' said Pitt mockingly, 'that gentlemen are day after day putting off the business of the nation and yet are

Pitt addressing the House of Commons, by Karl-Anton Hickel.

apprehensive that this putting off may be construed to mean delay.' Members began to tire of the wordy protestations of an opposition which did not have the courage to oppose. The last of these protestations, a long Representation to the King which was debated on 8 March, passed by only one vote; and the next day the Mutiny Act went through unopposed. In less than three months Pitt had defeated the House of Commons and shown that government in England was still the business of the King. Two weeks later George III dissolved Parliament and made ready to show his enemies that he could command a new House of Commons as effectively as he had commanded the old.

Only two members spoke out on 9 March as the Fox–North opposition let the Mutiny Act through in embarrassed silence. One was Sir Matthew White Ridley, a coal-owning country gentleman from Northumberland who sat for Newcastle upon Tyne, as his father had done before him, and who had always upheld the family tradition of independence in politics. In many ways he was typical of those independent men who had looked up to the Pitt family for nearly fifty years as their champions against the unscrupulous oligarchs in London. The other was Thomas Powys, an independent country gentleman like Sir Matthew but a much more active one politically: he had already played a central role in negotiations initiated by the independents and aimed at bringing Pitt and Fox together. These negotiations had failed, as had every other effort made by the independents to assert their importance in politics at this critical juncture. Most independents were sensible enough to shrug their shoulders and admit defeat, but Ridley and Powys were made of sterner stuff. They stormed and ranted at their fellow members, accusing them of betraying their trust and allowing the Crown to trample on their essential rights. Powys declared that the liberties won nearly a century before, at the time of the 'Glorious Revolution' of 1688, were now being abandoned: after ninety-five years of freedom the Commons were leading their fellow-countrymen back into the shadow of royal despotism. Ridley admitted that 'a misguided people had been taught to desert their natural guardians and fly for protection to the Crown', but this did not seem to him to be sufficient reason for the Commons to give up their ancient rights and privileges. The people would soon come to regret what they had done. They might connive at the discredit and degradation of the House of Commons but they would not easily find a substitute for it.

In a sense Ridley and Powys were right. The constitutional arrangements made in 1688 had never been very satisfactory. They represented not so much a plan for governing the country as an admission that it could not be governed at all. For nearly a hundred years the greater part of the functions of government had been carried out not at a central but at a local level: noblemen and gentlemen in the counties, aldermen and freemen in the towns, had held sway over their inferiors with very little reference to the wishes of the government in London. That government might pass new laws but it could not get them obeyed unless the local magnates saw fit to enforce them. As for national policy, that too had had to be adjusted to the caprices and uncertainties of the parliamentary system: Chatham's disastrous policy towards America in 1767, one of the prime causes of the American revolution, had been in part the result of a government defeat in the Commons which had cut the proposed rate of direct taxation by a quarter. Now the moment of reckoning had come. The English had put liberty before order for ninety-five years and they had won and lost an empire as a result. They had also developed a whole new way of life, an expanding economy which might have grown out of liberty but still needed ordering – needed it far more desperately and far more decisively than it needed the genial incompetence which was the product of independent local potentates and an independent House of Commons. The liberties of England as Ridley and Powys understood them were quite simply out of date. And by a savage stroke of irony it was the scion of the house of Pitt, the Patriot turned bureaucrat, who was to turn those liberties into new and carefully controlled channels.

George III and his political managers did not share Ridley's certainty about the attitude of the 'misguided people'. The King wrote to his bankers to borrow £24,000 at five per cent the day before he dissolved Parliament; and as the election campaign gathered momentum larger and larger sums were poured in, both by the Crown and by the East India Company. Government agents had been sounding out constituencies for some time past, 'nibbling at boroughs as well as at men' as one infuriated opposition member had put it, and Pitt had had a difficult time explaining away these activities. His vehement denials carried less conviction in this matter than they did on the issue of 'secret influence', since the chief culprit was well known and his actions could easily be traced. John Robinson, the King's principal political manager, was the man in question: he had prepared the original estimates Pitt had seen in secret in December and he was reporting regularly on every development that might influence the coming elections. When Sheridan made veiled references to government corruption and was challenged to name the person responsible he replied that he would not do so because it would be invidious; but he insisted that if he had wished to name him he could easily have done so 'as soon as you could say Jack Robinson'. When the polls opened at the end of March the efficiency of Robinson and his counterparts in the East India Company was soon made clear. News of Pittite victories and Foxite defeats continued to pour in all through April and in the new House of Commons, which met on 18 May, Pitt had a majority of well over a hundred. Misguided or not, the people – or at any rate those of them who had sufficient property or status to be electors – had pronounced very decisively in favour of those prerogative powers which Pitt had described as such an essential part of their rights.

The line between the powers of the Crown and the wishes of the people was as blurred in the details of the General Election as it had been in Pitt's piece of constitutional doctrine. No eighteenth-century government had ever lost a General Election, but few had won one as decisively and dramatically as this. The efficiency of the King's political machine, combined with the efforts of the East India Company and the careful manipulation of public opinion by government propaganda, provided part of the reason but it could by no means explain everything. It could not explain why Foxite candidates did so badly in constituencies where public opinion counted for most, such as the counties and some of the larger towns, while they picked up votes in the pocket boroughs they were supposed to despise. Nor did it explain why Pitt's propaganda was so successful while that of his opponents was for the most part self-defeating. And in any case the election was no more corrupt than many of its predecessors: the King himself spent little more than half of what he had paid out for the General Election of 1780, while East India intervention was on nothing like the scale that had been expected. Pitt the reformer had been swept back to power by the corrupt and unreformed electoral system, but in a way that suggested a genuine movement of public opinion as well as the effective mobilisation of traditional patronage resources. The only trouble was that the public opinion was rooted firmly in the past while Pitt had his eyes on

Downing Street in the early nineteenth century, by J. C. Buckley.

the future. Even as he propelled his King and his country into one dramatic change after another he would have to remember that they saw him as their shield and buckler against all the things they hated and feared. And the thing they hated above all else, the thing they feared even more than they feared Fox and North, was change itself.

Few of these tensions and dilemmas appeared during the triumphant summer of 1784. George III was studiously affable to his enthusiastic young minister, complimenting him on his gentlemanly behaviour in the Commons and passing on to him with royal condescension the fruits of his own long experience of politics. The King entered his forty-seventh year a week after Pitt entered his twenty-sixth. The royal birthday, on 4 June, was celebrated with due ceremony both at the Court of St James's and at the royal foundation of Eton, where the boys had already turned the King's anniversary to their own uses; but the ministerial birthday on 28 May was passed over in silence. Pitt was too busy with the fruits of his own year of victory to pause too long over the fact that he had himself been a product of his father's comparable year. His father had won an empire which had never been properly administered and which had consequently produced revolution on one side of the world and scandalous misgovernment on the other. The scandals of Britain's rule in India had still to be brought under control, while the problem of trade with the Americans and their European allies, the economic and commercial aftermath of the American revolution, had still to be resolved. Pitt was already immersed in what he later called the most important objective of his political life – 'to unite and connect what yet remains of our shattered empire'.

It was an unparalleled task, amounting to nothing short of the complete reconstruction of the world which had been turned on its head at Yorktown. Viewed from 10 Downing Street – already the recognised home of First Lords of the Treasury, even though they were not yet called prime ministers – things looked familiar enough. Boxes left the house filled with papers for the King's consideration and they returned with brief but gracious indications of royal approval. Round the corner, within the rambling precincts of the old Palace of Westminster, the Commons crowded into St Stephen's Chapel in order to hear Pitt explain the measures which the King wished them to approve. The balance between King and Parliament, the vital constitutional principle which Pitt

Holwood House in Kent was bought by Pitt in 1785.

claimed to have vindicated, assumed visible and tangible form in these two interlocking halves of his life. But the truth was that the two halves did not make a whole. His relations with George III, essential though they were as the ultimate source of all his power, only took up a very small part of Pitt's time; and during the first three and a half years of his administration Parliament only sat for just over four hundred days. In theory the new minister should have had ample time to relax and enjoy himself in the way that most of his predecessors had done. He could have established himself as a great landowner, reared a family, lived a fashionable life in London. Yet he did none of these things. He told his mother in August 1784 that he thought of himself now as a country gentleman, but this was only because he had managed to rent a house on Putney Heath; and when he actually bought a house the following year at Holwood in Kent, a mile or so from his father's old house at Hayes, he found that he had too little time to carry out all the landscape gardening and 'improvements' that he planned. London life went the same way: his payments to Goostree's, which had amounted to £444 in 1783, fell to £100 in 1784 and seem to have stopped altogether in the following year. Domestic expenditure, on the other hand, ran at a very high level. Between July 1784 and July 1785 he spent £864 on wine, half of that total being accounted for by 2,410 bottles of port at just under two shillings a bottle and 854 bottles of madeira at just over four shillings. Robert Smith, a banker friend whom he asked to look over his affairs in 1785, found that he already had unpaid debts amounting to £8,000. There was something else in William Pitt's life other than the normal pursuits of his class, other than the excitement of parliamentary debate and the tedium of attendance upon the King. It was something that kept him at home and yet prevented him from running his domestic affairs properly, something that kept his wine bills high and his engagement book empty, something that made it easier for tradesmen to cheat him than for friends to invite him out to dinner.

That something was the business of government. Gone were the days of the lordly amateurs, the nonchalant and well-bred ministers who delegated to clerks and scribes the task of drafting documents which would satisfy both King and Parliament. If the shattered empire was indeed to be 'united and connected' there would have to be hard work as well as heady slogans. In the spacious days before the American revolution political life in general – and Patriot political life in particular – had been largely a matter of reiterating lofty convictions which were expected to solve all problems if only they were held to with sufficient consistency and high-mindedness. Chatham himself had once said that he would never be 'a proposer of plans' but would wait for the sense of the nation to be expressed in Parliament and then advise the King to follow it. Chatham's son, however, had to be not merely a proposer of plans but a promoter of planning and an overseer of planners. He had to be the creator and animator of an entirely new kind of administrative machine. It could be said of him, as it was later to be said of his great opponent Napoleon Bonaparte, that he had come to substitute an age of work for an age of talk.

4

THE BUSINESS OF GOVERNMENT

PITT'S WINE BILLS reflected public problems as well as private predilections. The 2,410 bottles of port that he and his guests got through in 1784-5 were smaller than present-day bottles and wine itself was somewhat lighter; but at less than two shillings a bottle it was still very good value compared with French wines which sold for three or four times as much even though they were considerably lower in alcoholic content. The laws which cut the duty on port and increased that on claret and other French wines dated from the days of the Glorious Revolution, when Portugal had been our ally against a King of France who seemed determined to overthrow parliamentary rule in England and restore the Stuarts. A man's drink had therefore become something of an indication of his politics: loyal Whig adherents of the House of Hanover raised their port glasses to the health of King George, while Tories were suspected of drinking surreptitiously to their 'king across the water' in French claret.

Certainly a great deal of claret was drunk in England, whether by Tories or not, and almost as much in Scotland. French brandy was also imported on a large scale: even the humblest farmer's wife regarded it as an essential ingredient for her cakes and puddings and party drinks. Few people were anxious to pay the full price for claret and brandy and so smuggled liquor always found a ready market. James Woodforde, a most respectable and pious country parson in Somerset, got his supplies regularly from 'Moonshine' John Buck, a local blacksmith who had taken up smuggling as a profitable sideline; and there were many people far more powerful and influential than James Woodforde or John Buck who had a vested interest in the smuggling industry. Even Sir Robert Walpole, the only eighteenth-century minister so far who had made a serious attempt to stop smuggling, had had dealings with smugglers himself in his private capacity and had made a useful profit out of them. The contrast between Pitt's 2,410 bottles of port at two shillings and his 572 bottles of claret at five shillings was not just a matter of personal taste. It was the outward and visible sign of a half-hidden world in which foreign policy, domestic affairs, government revenue and commercial policy were all involved. Just as the smuggling network epitomised the tradition of local independence at its most irresponsible, so the discrepancies between different rates of duty represented the worst aspects of the old protectionist system that bedevilled relations with America and Europe.

PREVIOUS PAGE Pitt portrayed as banker in a Gillray cartoon on the issue of paper money.

OPPOSITE Pitt's port wine glass.

OVERLEAF Smugglers and their loot.

It was not just 'brandy for the parson and 'baccy for the clerk' that were at stake. More than three-quarters of the government's revenue came from indirect taxes, from customs and excise duties levied on every conceivable commodity. While the wine and tobacco duties reflected traditional hostility towards France and a determination to provide protected markets for American produce, the duty on tea gave expression to a suspicious fear of enervating oriental luxuries. By the 1780s many writers were becoming seriously worried by the effects of tea-drinking on the working classes, whose natural vigour was apparently being undermined by this pernicious drug which so many of them seemed to prefer to good honest English beer. But while beer provided a wholesome alternative to the horrors of imported tea, the alternative to imported brandy was gin, a beverage which found little favour with anybody except the poor whose miseries it solaced and the farmers who found in the distilleries a useful market for grain which had gone bad. The social and ethical aspects of the problem, aspects which could not be neglected in this increasingly moralising and self-righteous age, were as tangled as the economic and political ones.

The figures which Pitt studied when he got down to serious work in the summer of 1784 showed that the national debt stood at just over £240 million, something like sixteen or seventeen times the government's annual revenue. Interest on the debt was running at about £8 million a year, well over half of each year's revenue. And expenditure, even now that the war had been over for more than a year, was still well in excess of revenue. There seemed to be only one conclusion to be drawn: the country was on the verge of bankruptcy. On all sides prophets of gloom talked of complete national collapse. The attempt to subdue the rebellious American colonists seemed to have undermined not merely Britain's position in the New World but her position as a whole: she had reduced herself to a state in which she could neither govern her remaining possessions, from the closest ones such as Ireland to the farthest ones such as India, nor adjust her affairs so as to be able to do without them. The freeholders and freemen who had signed the loyal addresses earlier in the year shared many of these fears, but in their more cheerful moments they tended to think that all the trouble was caused by two things: the wartime corruption they associated with Lord North and the peacetime corruption they associated with the Rockingham Whigs. Since

An engraving of Adam Smith from the portrait by John Kaye in 1790.

Pitt was free of both these taints it was assumed that he would somehow mend matters and avert the national catastrophe which threatened. It was also assumed, even more unreasonably, that he would be able to do so without offending against any of the nation's cherished freedoms and prejudices – the localism that made the smuggling industry possible, the chauvinism that kept out foreign goods, the resentment that refused to trade with the Americans, the tradition of liberty which saw as tyranny any increase of taxation – particularly direct taxation – in time of peace.

Pitt hoped to find an answer to this apparently insoluble problem in the new economic theories advanced by Adam Smith and his followers. Most of these radical thinkers looked to Shelburne rather than to Pitt as their political patron and in 1787, when it was said that 'Dr Smith was much with the ministry', one of his friends confessed that he was 'vexed that Pitt should have done so right a thing as to consult Smith'. Shelburne himself was very proud of his little gaggle of intellectual *protégés* and he was also very careful to maintain contacts with the new industrialists, the textile manufacturers of Lancashire and the Midlands and the hardware magnates of Birmingham, whose spectacular success seemed to underline the breakdown of old economic policies and the need for new ones. For these men had done well in precisely those conditions in which industry was supposed to do badly – the loss of protected markets in America, the unprecedented expansion of foreign industrial competition, the upsetting of business confidence by wartime credit crises. There was a whole new world struggling to be born, a world in which free trade would make possible increased production while increased production in its turn yielded tax levels far higher than those which had been squeezed so painfully out of the stunted structure of protectionist economics. And Shelburne intended to be the midwife for that new world. His careful cultivation of radical intellectuals and self-made industrialists was to pave the way for a triumphant political comeback.

Unfortunately for Shelburne and his hopes, the intellectuals could not be prevented from writing books and Pitt could not be prevented from reading them. Shelburne and Pitt had already worked together on free trade policies, when they had tried to make the peace treaty of 1783 the basis of a new commercial relationship both with America and with Europe; but it had been Shelburne's political career that had been crushed by the weight of that unpopular treaty, while Pitt had adroitly dodged the odium. Shelburne was not only distrusted by the party leaders: he was also distrusted now by George III, who considered that he ought to have stayed in office when defeated by the Fox–North coalition and defied its Commons majority in the way Pitt did some months later. The King was quick to sniff out treachery and political cowardice and slow to forgive those he considered guilty of these things. In his view Shelburne fell into the same category as Temple, the man who had urged him to desperate action in December 1783 and had then deserted

ABOVE Mining at Menai in 1780.

BELOW The processes of an iron foundry.

the new ministry after only three days. In November 1784 it was announced that the King was graciously pleased to raise both men to the rank of Marquis, Shelburne becoming Marquis of Lansdowne and Temple Marquis of Buckingham; and from that time forward it was made clear to them that their new status was intended to mark the end of their active political careers. There is nothing to suggest that Pitt actively encouraged the royal displeasure on this score, but he certainly did little to abate it. He saw no reason to welcome Lansdowne as a colleague just because he stood in need of the new ideas that Lansdowne had helped to formulate.

At first the attempts to apply the new ideas were ill-judged and only partially successful. Feeling against free trade with America was running very high, fed by Lord Sheffield's widely read *Observations on the Commerce of the American States*, and the various committees established by Pitt to consider the question reported unfavourably. It was not until 1787 that he was able to take the first real step towards reopening the American trade by setting up free ports in the British West Indies to act as *entrepôts*. A grandiose scheme for free trade with Europe, which involved commercial negotiations with countries right across the continent from Spain to Russia, had run itself into the ground by the end of 1785 and Pitt had to settle instead for a Commercial Treaty with France alone. This treaty, which was signed in 1786 and came into force the following year, provided for drastic reductions in duties on French wine coming into England and on English manufactured goods going into France. It could be seen as a partial success for Pitt's free trade policy but it could also be interpreted as something of a set-back. Pitt himself had made it clear earlier in the negotiations that he regarded an exclusive agreement with France as an obstacle, rather than an aid, to wider and eventually more advantageous free trade treaties. Certainly there was no love lost between the two governments: the French Royal Council did its best to force Pitt's hand by decrees against British trade and by hostile negotiations with other countries; while Pitt for his part showed in all his dealings with France a residuum of that violent anti-French feeling which had been his father's principal stock-in-trade.

Failures and frustrations in America and Europe were accompanied by outright defeats nearer home. Pitt's proposals for free trade with Ireland were accepted by the Irish Parliament in Dublin early in 1785 but encountered fierce opposition in England. Ireland's economic subjection to England was far harsher and more oppressive than anything the Americans had suffered: she was excluded from the colonial trade and she was forbidden to export woollen textiles either to England or to foreign countries. Similar restrictions crippled her agriculture and such industries as she had been able to develop, with the result that by 1785 conditions in Ireland were so grim that there was a real danger that she might 'go the way of America'. Pitt's friend the Duke of Rutland, whom he had sent to Ireland as Lord Lieutenant, reported that French agents were having considerable success in their attempts to push the Irish towards open rebellion. Free trade with Ireland was not just a matter of economic theory or fiscal policy, a pleasant luxury which might lead eventually to greater prosperity and higher revenue yields. It was a vital and immediate necessity without which the shattered empire might well become yet more shattered. But this did not stop the opposition from exploiting the fears of all those English landowners and industrialists who thought they were vulnerable to competition from Ireland. Lord Sheffield, who had already done so much to block free trade with America, was one of the chief organisers of this opposition campaign, which eventually forced Pitt into revising his proposals so radically that they became unacceptable to the Irish and had to be withdrawn altogether. Ireland's economic grievances and France's exploitation of them continued to be an anxiety and a reproach to the British government until they finally burst into open rebellion thirteen years later.

Pitt's other defeats during his first two years in office were concerned not so much with free trade itself as with the alterations and adjustments in taxation which had to accompany it. He wanted to lower the levels of indirect taxation, not merely in order to further the cause of international free trade, but also as a means of increasing total yield. He calculated – correctly, as it turned out – that lower rates of duty would cut the smugglers' profits and in the end kill smuggling far more effectively than harsh penalties and vigilant revenue officers could ever do. Vigilance was certainly not slackened – the customs and excise officials were backed up by eight regiments of soldiers and by naval forces that now had authority to board any vessel behaving suspiciously off the coast – but it was to be accompanied by a deliberate policy of lowering duties and thus reducing both the temptation to buy smuggled goods and the incentive to sell them. Tea, in particular, was nearly halved

The Irish House of Commons in 1780.

Ladies' headgear was among the new articles taxed by Pitt.

in price so that it was now possible to buy it legally at a lower price than had previously been charged for smuggled tea. The moralists might still be worried about the increasing decadence of a tea-drinking labouring class, but at least the evil of smuggling, and the violence and gang warfare which it brought with it, was at last on the decline.

The only snag about this policy was that new taxes had to be devised so that the government could maintain its revenue while it was waiting for the expected expansion of trade – and thus of tax yield – to work its way through. In order to pay for the reduction in tea duties Pitt revived the idea of a tax on windows; and this was generally admitted to be fair, even though it did lead to the construction of some unduly gloomy new buildings and to the disfigurement of some old ones that had to have their windows blocked up in order to avoid tax. Other taxes proposed in 1784 proved less popular and Pitt had to drop his plans to put a duty on coal and to charge licence fees for the planting of hops. A tax on ladies' ribbons also had to be drastically revised and Pitt began to acquire a reputation as a prudish young spoilsport who taxed other people's innocent pleasures not for the sake of the revenue – in many cases this was trifling – but because he was incapable of enjoying them himself. His tax on maidservants, laid before the House of Commons in 1785, led to a hilarious debate in which members vied with one another to produce elaborate innuendoes linking the minister's proposals with his alleged impotence. This was followed by a flood of comment by the caricaturists and the journalists, most of it a good deal less subtle and gentlemanly than the remarks made in Parliament. In the end the tax was accompanied by one on menservants as well and Pitt accepted a scheme to tax bachelors at a higher rate than married men. His fiscal policy continued, however, to be represented in the press as a priggish attack on pleasure. Taxes on hats and perfumes were followed by taxes on horses, playing-cards, hair powder, sporting dogs, clocks and watches and countless other articles.

All this provided admirable ammunition for the opposition, but it had little to do with the real nature of his financial achievements, which were in fact quite staggering. During his first eight years in office he raised government revenue by nearly fifty per cent, from £12½ million to £18½ million; and he did this not by his taxes on luxury goods, which often cost too much in collection to make them really worth while, but

An engraving of 1784 shows a farmer riding his cow to Stockport Market in defiance to Pitt's tax on horses.

by his carefully calculated reductions in indirect taxation, all of them aimed at increasing ultimate yield by encouraging the expansion of trade. His ideas were not original – quite apart from the theories of Adam Smith there were the reports of committees and commissions set up by previous governments, most of them pointing in the same direction – but the courage and persistence with which he carried them out should not be underestimated. In spite of the reverses he suffered over trade with America and with Ireland, in spite of the often factious opposition to the Commercial Treaty with France, he continued to work towards a well-defined aim. He intended to bring the indirect taxes down to a level where they would neither cripple trade nor encourage smuggling; and having done that he intended to make sure that they were collected in a way that minimised fraud, evasion and administrative costs.

The Customs House beside the Thames in London.

He intended, in fact, to establish what contemporaries called 'a general excise'.

Men of property had for many years been deeply suspicious of excise duties. Unlike customs dues, which were payable when goods entered the country, excise was charged when the article in question was taken 'out of bond' – that is, when it left the bonded excise warehouses into which it went on arrival. This meant that excise inspectors had to be employed to examine goods on sale, whether in shops or in taverns, to see whether they had the right markings that showed they had been through bond. It was a far more efficient system than customs and it could be applied to goods produced at home as well as those coming in from abroad. But it was universally hated because it was said that excise inspectors, with their right of entry into private premises, represented continental tyranny rather than British liberty. Fifty years earlier Sir Robert Walpole, probably the most skilful of all eighteenth-century ministers at the art of placating the touchiness of the country gentlemen in the House of Commons, had withdrawn an excise scheme rather than risk the fall of his administration. Pitt knew the risk he was running but he also knew that things had changed a lot since Sir Robert's day. 'I am just going to introduce a plan for excising wine,' he told his friend Rutland in April 1786, 'which, although it had nearly overthrown Sir Robert Walpole will, I believe, meet with very little difficulty.'

He was right. He not only got his wine excise through but he scored an even greater triumph with his Consolidation Act of 1787, which tidied up and rationalised the whole structure of indirect taxation. By 1790 he had extended the excise system to tobacco as well as alcohol, thus achieving everything that Walpole had attempted and achieving it with scarcely a ripple of opposition. When even the Whig leaders praised his efforts and complimented him on his fiscal skill there was not much that the country gentlemen could do but acquiesce. It was little more than twenty years since they had waged a turbulent and ultimately successful campaign against an excise on cider; and in this campaign they had had the powerful support of Chatham, who had denounced in ringing tones the excise inspectors whose powers flouted the ancient principle that an Englishman's home was his castle. Now Chatham's son was appointing such inspectors on an unprecedented scale. If this was Patriot politics, then patriotism had undergone a very remarkable change in the course of a single generation.

The key to this change lay not so much in the structure of taxation as in the structure of government itself. On the face of things this was a field in which Pitt had been pushing ahead with the Patriot programme of sinecure reform. In spite of the reductions made by the Whigs in 1782 there were still many hundreds of sinecure posts, jobs which were usually completely undemanding but which brought in large fees and other perquisites to their fortunate holders. Pitt made a great impression on the House of Commons, especially on the independent backbenchers, by refusing such a post himself at the very beginning of his administration: the Clerkship of the Pells fell vacant, worth £3,000 a year, and instead of taking it for himself he gave it to one of Shelburne's followers. Some of the older men among the independents may have remembered how Pitt's father, when he first came into office as Paymaster in 1746, had ostentatiously refused to milk his office for private profit in the way that had been customary up to that time. The son's gesture was even more effective because Colonel Barré, the Shelburne man in question, took the Clerkship in exchange for a pension of £3,200 a year which had been given him by the Rockingham Whigs and which had been sharply criticised. Pitt was able to demonstrate at one and the same time his own integrity and the murky dealings of at least two of his main rivals. This was just the kind of thing the country gentlemen liked, particularly since the country was saved £3,200 a year. Even more dramatic was the abolition in 1785 of the Auditors of the Imprests, offices so lucrative that their holders had to be paid £7,000 a year for life as compensation.

That £7,000 a year gave Pitt pause. If sums of that sort were to be doled out in respect of every sinecure that was suppressed it would turn sinecure reform into a very expensive gesture. And Pitt was not really interested in gestures any longer. He wanted a genuine improvement in the efficiency of government, not merely the plaudits of the independent men. He therefore turned away from the temptingly spectacular but really rather self-defeating business of sweeping sinecure reforms. Instead he let sinecures wither quietly away: when their holders died the offices were suppressed instead of being given to somebody else. At the same time steps were taken to inquire into the fees that sinecurists charged for their imaginary services. Burke, who after his efforts in 1782 tended to regard sinecure reform as his own preserve, mocked at Pitt's piecemeal methods and said that he was merely 'hunting in holes and corners'. But Pitt's methods worked, even though they took a long time to do so. And they worked at an administrative as well as at a political level: they made government more efficient as well as reducing the corruption that the independents were so worried about. For Pitt did not only abolish old offices: he also created new ones. Gentlemanly amateurs, men who saw their posts as rewards to be enjoyed, were replaced by professional civil servants who had a job to do and might well be dismissed if they did not do it. The new men were often of humbler origin, clerks utterly dependent on their wages rather than men of substance and position who could defy their masters. And they were normally paid salaries rather than fees. At long last the government of England was becoming a job to be done rather than an opportunity to be exploited.

It was for this reason that Pitt's gradual scaling down of sinecures was in reality a threat to those same independent men who were so ready to applaud it. For their whole position was based on the assumption that government, national as well as local, was a business for gentlemanly amateurs. Most of them were Justices of the Peace, unpaid magistrates who were responsible not merely for meting out some kind of rough justice at a local level but also for a certain amount of administrative work. When the Justices of the Peace for a particular county met in Quarter Sessions they were in theory a kind of county court, but in practice they formed something approaching a county council, an administrative rather than a judicial body. It seemed obvious to them that if either local or national government were entrusted to poor men on the make, instead of to men of property and substance like themselves who had no need to make a profit out of it, it would become increasingly corruptible and corrupted. Most of them failed to see that the scope and range of government activities, and the expertise needed to carry them out, had widened and deepened to such an extent that their own part-time and part-trained approach just would not do any longer. The magistrates for the London area, poised uncomfortably between the easy-going traditions of the local Justice and the complex problems of a capital city, were a case in point. Many independents agreed with Burke and the Whigs, who thought that the answer to London's problems was to appoint wealthier and more gentlemanly Justices, men less open to temptation. Pitt, on the other hand, found that the solution lay in making the magistracy, in London at least, into a properly paid profession whose members

The weight of Pitt's taxation was a popular grievance for the cartoonists.

received a salary sufficiently substantial to make bribes unnecessary and training worth while. He even tried, in 1785, to set up a police force for the metropolis; but this particular venture into positive and professional government was voted down in the Commons as an example of continental tyranny.

The Act establishing stipendiary magistrates in London was passed in 1792. By this time Pitt had lived down his early failures and uncertainties and he had five years of the reorganised system of customs and excise behind him, as well as the cumulative effect of nearly a decade of civil service reform. Smuggling had been dramatically reduced, trade was booming and the structure of government had been rationalised and streamlined so as to deal with the country's new prosperity and new problems. He had also set up a Sinking Fund, into which the government paid £1 million a year so that the Fund's commissioners could buy up government stock and thus eventually redeem – so it was hoped – the National Debt that had seemed so enormous and so threatening in 1784. Like so many of his ideas, the Sinking Fund was borrowed from one of

Lansdowne's tame intellectuals, Dr Richard Price. By February 1792, when he came to review his achievements in his budget speech, Pitt could justly claim that he had brought the country from defeat and demoralisation to a new era of prosperity. He did not fail to pay tribute to the industrialists and businessmen whose 'circulation and increase of capital' had helped to make all this possible; but it was clear that his new approach to the problems of government had provided an administrative framework for economic activity, a framework whose efficiency and professionalism had not been seen before. He had regularly consulted business interests, setting up once again the Board of Trade – which Burke had abolished in his 1782 reforms – and calling before it representatives of all the interests liable to be affected by his policies. The new world of commerce and industry had not always been impressed by him: the General Chamber of Manufacturers, formed in the early 1780s to oppose his linen and calico excise and his Irish trade proposals, had bitterly resented the disdain with which this son of an earl had treated honest tradesmen and industrialists who could have bought him out several times over. In spite of the growth of bureaucracy, in spite of the country gentlemen's resentment of London and its commercial tentacles, it remained true that Pitt was primarily the representative of a landed class whose power was supplemented, rather than supplanted, by the changes which were later to be dubbed 'the industrial revolution'.

Within a year of Pitt's optimistic speech the supremacy of the landed class, together with the attendant powers of its capitalistic outriders, were challenged from across the Channel. On 1 February 1793 the French Republic declared war on Great Britain. Having had nine fat years of peace in which to build up his new structure of government, Pitt had now to face the lean years of war which were to test it. Some of his favourite schemes broke under the strain – the Sinking Fund, for instance, soon became an absurdity as the government borrowed money at high rates of interest and then gave it to the Fund's commissioners so that they could redeem debts which were at a much lower rate – but the bureaucracy as a whole survived. If anything, the strains of war rendered it more necessary than before. Even on the domestic front the need for professional administrators and centralised government was revealed more and more clearly. The appalling conditions of the mid-1790s, when economic depression and

Liberty! Liberty! and no Excise! Huzza!
OPPOSITION
MINISTRY
JOHN-BULL Baited by the DOGS

An anti-taxation cartoon on the occasion of a petition for the repeal of the tobacco duty in 1790. The hounds chasing John Bull are identified by their collars. Pitt urges them on while George Rose paints a new name over the Treasury.

high unemployment were aggravated by soaring food prices, put an intolerable strain on the existing resources of local government. The Justices did their best, but even the most well-meaning and ingenious of their efforts – such as the notorious Speenhamland system of 1795, whereby wages were supplemented from the poor rates – merely made matters worse. As if in token of their surrender and admission of defeat the independent men in the Commons let through in 1800, without so much as a murmur of opposition, a proposal to take a census of the country's population. Half a century earlier they had thrown out such a scheme contemptuously, denouncing it in terms similar to those used by Chatham about the cider excise scheme. It was continental tyranny, they said, an invasion of local independence and a preparation for an unprecedented extension of the powers of central government. So it was, but by 1800 it had become unavoidable. Pitt's new concept of the nature of government had come to stay.

Meanwhile Pitt himself had come to be generally regarded as a typical bureaucrat, a cold and humourless administrator who disdained the healthy rough-and-tumble of political life. It was perhaps unfortunate for him that his administration should have coincided with the greatest and also the most vicious period in the history of English political caricature; but even allowing for this there is still much significance in the treatment he received from the cartoonists. Earlier ministers had usually been shown as straightforward villains, plotting constantly with corrupt colleagues to seize power and use it for their own evil ends. Pitt, on the other hand, was seldom represented as a plotter and never as a simple uncomplicated villain. There seemed to be nobody for him to plot with: his cabinet colleagues, if they featured in the popular prints at all, were mere subordinates. And it was seldom suggested that his motives were those of ordinary rogues and plotters – greed, corruption, love of power, desperate designs. Even the caricaturists seemed to recognise that he was above such things, that his sins if he had any were the colder sins of pride and arrogance and self-righteousness. His tall and unlovable figure stalks through the prints of the time, upturned nose absurdly exaggerated in its disdain and outstretched hand usually at the elbow of John Bull or George III, pointing out in schoolmasterly fashion what is good for them. If William Pitt was indeed the first prime minister of England, the first minister who towered sufficiently above his colleagues to deserve that as yet unofficial title, then it was the cartoonists who made him so.

The truth was somewhat different. His correspondence with the King shows that he survived not because he told George III what was good for him but because he usually contrived to tell him what he wanted to hear. The King's letters are those of a man who considers that he is in charge of policy and is graciously pleased to approve what his comparatively young and inexperienced minister has done. This has led some historians to suggest that the King really was in control and that Pitt was for many years little more than an apprentice learning his craft from his royal master. Closer examination of all the evidence, especially of the papers bearing on financial and administrative problems, shows that this was not so. Nobody other than Pitt could control these aspects of policy because nobody else really understood them in all their bewildering detail. Further down the chain of command were men like George Rose, Secretary to the Treasury, who shared Pitt's absorbing interest in such things; but at cabinet level there was no one. Most of Pitt's lordly colleagues were conscientious and honourable men, very different from the colourless nonentities who appeared occasionally in the public prints and have since appeared – even more occasionally – in the history books. The Duke of Richmond, who sat in the cabinet as Master General of the Ordnance, was passionately concerned about national defence and incurred considerable and unjustified unpopularity in trying to improve it. The Duke of Leeds, Foreign Secretary in 1791, resigned rather than abandon at Pitt's behest a policy which he thought right. But in the end such men were at a hopeless disadvantage because they could not defend their policies in the House of Commons and because they seldom had a proper grasp of the logistic and administrative and financial consequences of what they were doing. George III might consult them – and he regularly did so, because he was intensely jealous of his royal powers and wished to show that he and not Pitt was the final arbiter – but in practice he could very seldom accept their advice if it ran counter to what his First Lord of the Treasury pronounced to be possible.

Pitt's ascendancy over the Commons, like his ascendancy over his colleagues and over the King, owed as much to his grasp of administrative detail as to his oratorical powers. In this, as in so many things, he was the nephew of George

Grenville rather than the son of the Earl of Chatham. He copied his father's aloofness, stalking to his seat in the chamber without glancing either to right or to left, without attempting to make himself in the least affable to the men whose support he sought. Yet he never quite won the kind of awed respect that Chatham had been able to command. Whereas the father had dominated men by lifting them out of themselves, making them feel that under his leadership they were greater and nobler than they had been before, the son put them firmly in their places and explained to them with careful but slightly condescending patience the governmental mysteries that he alone seemed able to penetrate. Only in his later years, when the perils of war lifted political life on to a new and more emotional level, did he come to be accepted as one who led the Commons instead of merely lecturing to them.

At the heart of it all there was a loneliness that was both palliated and perpetuated by unremitting hard work. Within his own family circle he was able to relax and be himself, but the pressure of government business meant less and less frequent visits to Burton Pynsent, the real centre of the family circle and the home of the mother whom he adored. In 1785 family life and official life overlapped for a few months when his sister Harriot came to act as his hostess at Downing Street; but she got married in September of that year and in 1786 she died after giving birth to her only child, a little girl who was also called Harriot. Pitt was deeply affected by her death for, as a mutual acquaintance once said, ''twas a pity she was his sister, for no other woman in the world was suited to be his wife'. It was a remark that gave considerable insight, perhaps more than its author realised, into the nature of the Pitt family circle. Not until 1803, when his niece Lady Hester Stanhope made her home with him, did he have anyone who came near taking Harriot's place. The Duchess of Gordon, who acted as his hostess from 1787 to 1790, was a great help to him politically and socially, giving gay supper parties which made the house in Downing Street into something more than an office; but she does not seem to have played any significant part in his emotional life.

OPPOSITE Lady Hester Stanhope, Pitt's niece, was a most unconventional woman who smoked a pipe and wore eccentric clothes. After Pitt's death she left England and spent the rest of her life as a self-appointed pundit on Mount Lebanon.

There were very few pressures, either emotional or physical, that could break down Pitt's icy self-control. When he had to have a tumour removed from his cheek in 1786 he refused to have his hands tied and underwent the operation without moving. The surgeon is said to have commented that he had

never, in all his practice, met such fortitude before. Eleanor Eden, the only woman outside his own family whom Pitt ever loved, either never knew or never revealed just what were the 'decisive and insurmountable obstacles' which he said prevented him from proposing marriage to her. George Rose, who was with Pitt when he received the unexpected news of his mother's death, saw the defences begin to crack but gave no hint of what lay behind them. All he would say was that 'Mr Pitt talked a good deal to me respecting the death of his mother and of feelings awakened by that event'. Those who were sufficiently intimate to share his drinking bouts were even more careful. Henry Dundas, for many years his drinking companion and perhaps his closest friend, never gave any indication as to what confidences the wine may have brought forth. Henry Addington, who graduated from boyhood friend to valued companion before he eventually became Pitt's political rival, was one of the few people who were permitted to sit on at the table sober while Pitt and Dundas drank: he did his best to moderate the drinking and when it was taking place at his own house he even tried, usually in vain, to withhold supplies. But he was also one of the very few people, as Lord Buckingham later pointed out somewhat maliciously, who deliberately destroyed all the letters Pitt wrote to him. If this loneliest of prime ministers did indeed have a secret then it was well kept. Posterity has accepted him, and will probably have to continue to accept him, as a man for whom the business of government was a passion and not a refuge.

5

THE GAME OF POLITICS

FINANCIAL AND ADMINISTRATIVE SKILLS, however wide their scope and however industrious their application, could not of themselves ensure the survival of an administration in the 1780s. There had to be political skill as well, the rare and God-given talent to exploit issues as they arose and to exploit them in such a way that one's own conduct appeared enlightened and honourable and disinterested while that of one's opponents seemed to be inspired by dark and devious motives. Pitt had shown his abilities in this direction in 1783 when he brought up parliamentary reform in order to split Fox from North; but his skills had been well matched by those of North himself, who had argued with unparalleled ingenuity that Pitt's proposed reforms were in fact reactionary and would increase still further the preponderance of the landed men over the commercial classes. Now that he was in power Pitt would have to show even greater ingenuity and agility if he was to keep the initiative and prevent his government from becoming a mere franking machine for changes for which his opponents took the credit.

India presented a particularly tricky problem. Anybody who had studied developments there – as Pitt had done, conscientiously and methodically – was almost certain to reach two main conclusions. The first was that the government must exercise some degree of supervision over the operations of the East India Company and the second was that it would be politically dangerous and administratively impossible to take over those operations altogether. When all the political capital that could be made had been made, when all the excited talk of chartered rights and the cornering of patronage had died down, there still remained the harsh fact that under existing conditions, with communications and administrative techniques in the state they were, day-to-day rule in India could not be carried out by a government many thousands of miles away. Pitt's East India Act of 1784, based on the Bill he had been prevented from carrying earlier that year, therefore gave the Company's officials in India much greater freedom of action than they would have had under Fox's Bill. This solved the administrative problem reasonably well, just as the other provisions of the Act solved the patronage problem by denying to the India Board the entrenched powers that Fox's Board would have had; but it did not solve the undoubted problem of misgovernment in India itself. India had been misgoverned for many hundreds of years: in this respect, as in so many others, she had conquered

PREVIOUS PAGE A cartoon of 1793 showing Pitt steering the ship of state between the rock of revolution and the whirlpool of royal despotism. The boat is pursued by Priestley, Fox and Sheridan, who were regarded as advocates of the French Revolution.

her conquerors. When the East India Company took over the powers of the Indian princes it had to take over, whether it liked it or not, some of their corrupt and often cruel methods. And in England, where there was already intense dislike of the newly enriched East India men, there was much political capital to be made by anybody who could prick the nation's conscience and make it march alongside the nation's prejudices in order to indict the Company's whole position in India.

The same explosive mixture of newly awakened conscience and freshly confirmed prejudice could be seen in the sudden concern Englishmen evinced over slavery and the slave-trade. For many years a small band of devoted humanitarians had been trying to expose the horrors of life on the American plantations and in the slave-ships that plied between Africa and the New World. They had had little success: men and women in the eighteenth century accepted the fact of human suffering as a necessary and perhaps even beneficent part of God's unfathomable ways. In any case, thousands of paupers and convicts were shipped across the Atlantic in conditions not much better than those of the slave-ships and to indentured service which might well amount to lifelong slavery – especially if they were foolish enough to run away, in which case their term of service could be extended by one month for every two hours they were at liberty. But when the War of American Independence suddenly transformed the slave-owners from brothers across the sea into rebels and traitors, Negro slavery became an issue. Not much was said about white servitude, because this would have made a tyrant out of every parish officer who had ever tried to get rid of a pauper without too much trouble; but the newly discovered scandal of black slavery could be loaded almost exclusively on to American shoulders and so became a political as well as a moral consolation. It was comforting to picture colonial enemies in America as heartless sadists with slaves cowering at their feet, just as it was comforting to picture envied East India Company magnates as practised torturers, extorting vast sums from begums and other Indian dignitaries by violence or the threat of violence.

There was a good deal of cant in all this. Crusty old John Byng, stumping about the English countryside and noting the desperate plight to which enclosures and other economic changes had reduced the labouring poor, was probably right to remind the 'pitiers of money-begums and free-ers of black slaves' that they should also concern themselves with suffering

Negroes for Sale.

A Cargo of very fine ſtout Men and Women, in good order and fit for immediate ſervice, juſt imported from the Windward Coaſt of Africa, in the Ship Two Brothers.— *Conditions are one half Caſh or Produce, the other half payable the firſt of January next, giving Bond and Security if required.*

The Sale to be opened at 10 *o'Clock each Day, in* Mr. Bourdeaux's *Yard,* at *No.* 48, *on the Bay.*

May 19, 1784. JOHN MITCHELL.

Thirty Seaſoned Negroes

To be Sold for Credit, at Private Sale.

AMONGST which is a Carpenter, nene of whom are known to be diſhoneſt.

Alſo, to be ſold for Caſh, a regular bred young Negroe Man-Cook, born in this Country, who ſerved ſeveral Years under an exceeding good French Cook abroad, and his Wife a middle aged Waſher-Woman, (both very honeſt) and their two Children. *Likewiſe*, a young Man a Carpenter.

For Terms apply to the Printer.

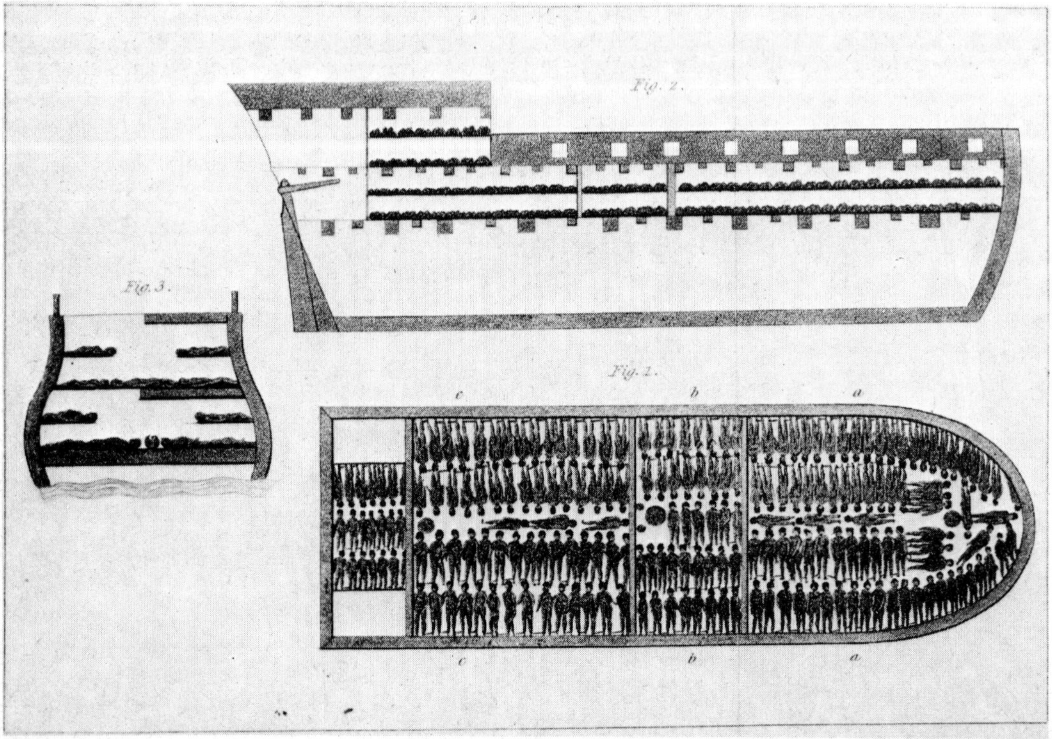

OPPOSITE The interior of a slave ship.

RIGHT On arrival in America the Negroes were put up for sale.

BELOW The design for a slave-carrying ship allowed only lying space for the cargo.

Fig. 2.

Fig. 3.

Fig. 1.

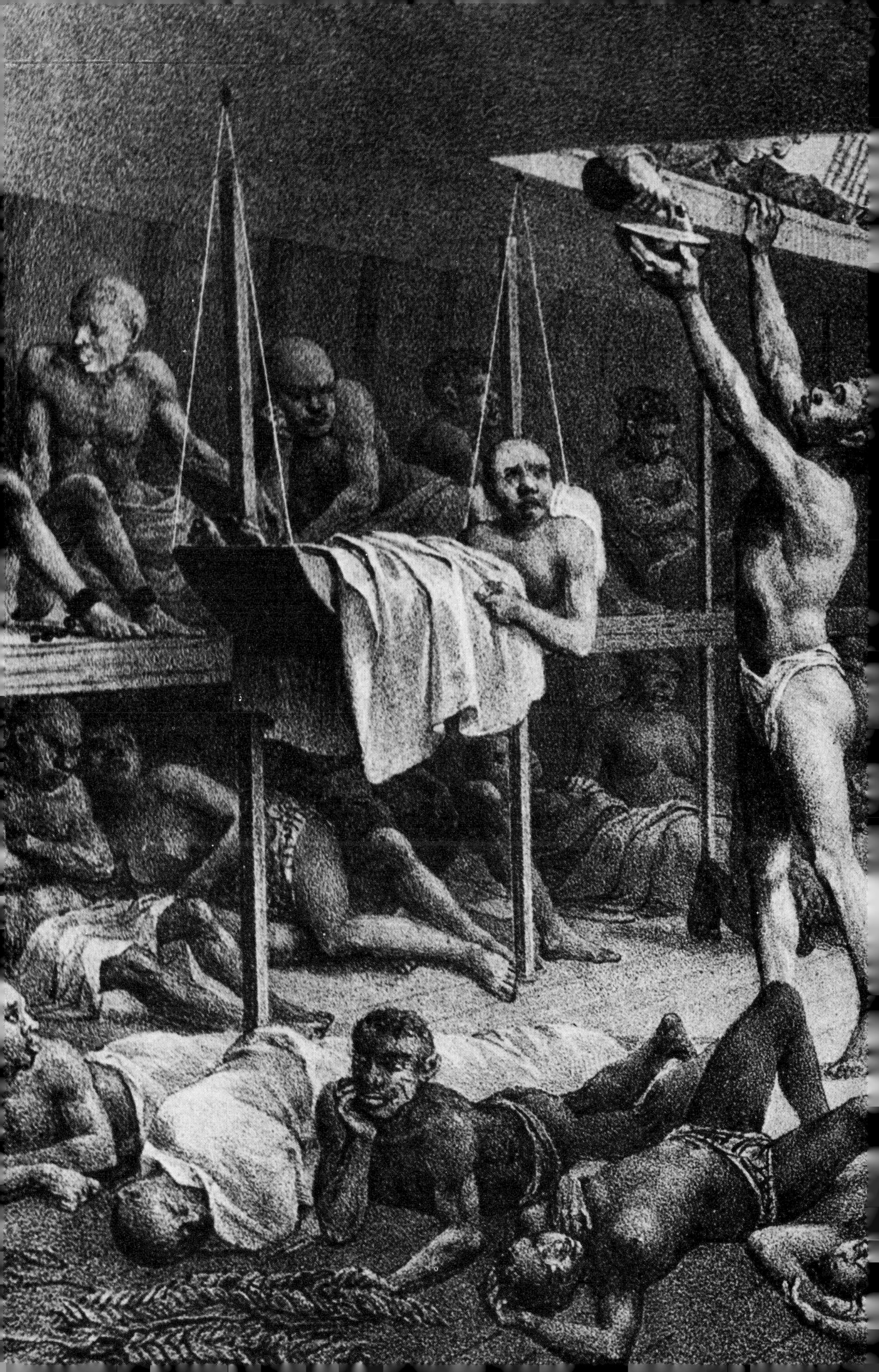

nearer home. But it remained true that in the existing climate of opinion there was more political advantage to be gained by exploiting public concern over India and the slave-trade than by reminding propertied men in England of the human problems which they were creating on their own doorsteps. Yet there were political dangers as well, especially for a minister in Pitt's position. Among the commercial classes, whose powerful opposition his Irish proposals and his taxation schemes were already arousing, there were influential vested interests determined to block any attempt to abolish the very lucrative slave-trade. Within the East India Company, whose general support for government was essential because it lent money to

Warren Hastings on his arab, after Stubbs.

the Treasury on a large scale, there were complex rivalries which meant that any attack on individual Company officials in India could produce dangerous cross-currents of support and opposition which might capsize any government that got caught in them. George III – upon whose favour Pitt's whole position still ultimately depended – was highly suspicious of those who made use of moral indignation and supposed humanitarianism to endanger such imperial possessions as he still had left. 'As to myself,' he told Pitt, 'I own I do not think it possible in that country to carry on business with the same moderation that is suitable to an European civilised nation.' As the scandals mounted and charges of corruption and cruelty were made against the rulers of India, the King reminded his ministers again and again that they must concern themselves with the stability of the East India Company's stocks on the London market rather than with the morality of its rule in India itself.

In 1785 the East India Company's first Governor General, Warren Hastings, arrived back in London. There were ugly rumours about the atrocities he was supposed to have committed and the vast sums he was supposed to have obtained by extortion; and when he challenged his accusers to substantiate their charges they laid articles for his impeachment before the House of Commons. The revival of the ancient procedure of impeachment was a reminder to the House of its great and glorious days during the previous century, when it had been able to bring down ministers of the King by drawing up charges of impeachment against them and requiring the House of Lords, as the highest court of the realm, to sit in judgment upon them. The trial of Warren Hastings, which opened in Westminster Hall on 13 February 1788, acted at first as a tonic and a stimulant to a House of Commons which was still smarting from the humiliation inflicted upon it by Pitt and the King four years earlier; but as the proceedings dragged on – Hastings was eventually acquitted in 1795 – the feeling of ancient rights vindicated and inhuman wrongs brought to book gave way to a conviction that the whole ponderous business was merely an excuse for the prosecution of private vendettas. The leaders of the opposition, especially Fox and Burke and Sheridan, had taken a prominent part in the affair: it was they who had first attacked Hastings in 1785 and who had managed the whole impeachment from then on. There was probably an element of sincerity in what they did – Burke, in particular, was passionately convinced of Hastings's guilt and believed himself

The trial of Warren Hastings in Westminster Hall dragged on for seven years before he was at last acquitted.

Lord Thurlow is shown riding George III and whipping back the hounds who had set upon Hastings. The sentinels appear to be Pitt and Lord Sydney.

to be the voice of mankind's conscience in this matter – but there was also an element of calculation. It had seemed very exciting at the beginning to pose as the guardians of both liberty and humanity, the defenders alike of the ancient rights of the House of Commons and of the wronged millions on the Indian continent. But by the end of the affair it was clear that the political instincts of George III had been sounder than those of Fox and Burke.

Pitt for his part behaved with considerable skill. When the charges against Hastings were first aired in the Commons in the spring of 1786 there was a general impression that the Pitt administration would defend him: it had, after all, established itself in power with the help of his friends in the East India Company and in face of opposition from those who now attacked him. And the government spokesmen did indeed secure the rejection of the first charge at the beginning of June. Then, a fortnight later, Pitt astonished the whole political world and shocked his royal master by voting in favour of the second charge and thus in effect making the impeachment possible. George III accepted, though with a certain grim reluctance, the explanation that Pitt gave: he had genuinely believed Hastings's policies to have been oppressive, even though they might have been justified by necessity, and therefore he had felt himself bound to vote for the impeachment. Others were more sceptical than the King. Some felt that Pitt was jealous of Hastings, others that he was influenced by his friend and colleague Henry Dundas, who supported the impeachment. It could even be argued that Pitt had calculated that the charge would be rejected by the House in any case and that it was therefore safe for him to make a moral gesture, to show that he was a humanitarian at heart and the enemy of oppressive Company officials even when he owed his position to their support. Only a few close friends such as William Wilberforce – with whom he had a hurried consultation during the debate, expressing his horror at the revelations that were being made – believed that he had acted sincerely out of a genuine repugnance for what Hastings had apparently done. And as the impeachment dragged on year after year, discrediting the opposition leaders and making Pitt's own position stronger as a result, there was an increasing tendency to credit him with far-sighted political acumen rather than reckless moral sincerity.

Over the other great humanitarian issue of the time, the movement for the abolition of the slave-trade, William Pitt's sincerity was unquestionable. Once again it was Wilberforce who was in his confidence and who was in the end to take over the leadership of the campaign. The two men talked over the matter in 1787, under an oak tree in the grounds of Holwood, an estate in Kent where Pitt had gone bird's-nesting as a boy and which he had now bought for himself. By the end of the year he was convinced not only that the trade should be ended but also that it could be ended, given skilful tactics and positive governmental action. 'The more I reflect upon it,' he wrote, 'the more anxious and impatient I am that the business should be brought as speedily as possible to a point.' He arranged for the Privy Council to begin an investigation into the trade and he authorised the British envoy in Paris to sound out the French government to see if it would agree to a joint abnegation of the trade by the two countries. He even agreed, when Wilberforce fell ill in the spring of 1788, to move himself the Commons resolution against the trade which his friend had intended to move. This very tentative resolution, calling only for a

William Wilberforce.

preliminary inquiry into the trade, got through so easily that opposition politicians, wise after the event, accused Pitt of being over-cautious and of crusading with weapons so blunt that they cast doubt upon his zeal and upon his motives. In fact, however, it was a very real fight and Pitt's caution in entering into it sprang from understanding rather than from cowardice. In the summer, after he had helped to carry in the Commons a Bill making some small improvements in the conditions in the slave-ships, some of his own cabinet colleagues who sat in the Lords threatened to throw the measure out of that House. Pitt told them icily that if they did he would bring it up again. 'If it fails then,' he wrote, 'the opposers of it and myself cannot continue members of the same government and I mean to state this distinctly to the cabinet before the House meets tomorrow.' It was one of the earliest of his resignation threats and also one of the bravest: it was by no means certain that the King regarded him as indispensable or shared his views, rather than those of his noble colleagues, on this issue. The threat worked and the Bill in question became law; but on the wider question of abolition itself the entrenched position of the slave trading interest became steadily stronger, gaining support both inside and outside the cabinet, and Pitt's own tactics became more and more cautious. Wilberforce proposed abolition year after year and Pitt made some eloquent and undoubtedly sincere speeches in support of it; but he studiously avoided any more cabinet crises and any suggestion of making abolition into an official government policy. In April 1792, after a passionate speech in which Pitt scathingly compared his contemporaries' contemptuous attitude to African 'barbarism' with the attitude of the ancient Romans to Britain herself, the abolitionist cause was effectively stifled by a delaying resolution which had the effect of keeping the trade going for another fifteen years. By the time it was eventually abolished, in 1807, Pitt was dead. Wilberforce, who was born in the same year as Pitt, lived on to see not only the abolition of the slave-trade but also the ending of slavery itself, throughout the British dominions, in 1833. The exertions of the single-minded campaigner, devoted to one cause and contemptuous of political manoeuvre, were perhaps in the end less wearing than those of the politician and statesman who had to cut down idealism and fit it into the harsh confines of reality.

The confines of reality, in this as in every other proposed reform of the period, were dictated by the pressures of war. The point about the debates of April 1792, the reason why they introduced fifteen years of reaction after five years of apparently hopeful reforming agitation, was that they were the last debates on this issue that took place in peacetime. Britain and France had been politely edging round one another ever since 1787, each determined that the other should be the first to abolish this very profitable trade; and when the two countries went to war in 1793 the chances of ending it were drastically reduced – especially since France in 1793 was ruled by a republican and revolutionary regime which seemed, in British eyes at any rate, to be the supporter and abettor of all manner of innovation and rebellion, whether by black slaves or by white agitators. The war against revolutionary France, and later against the France of the Emperor Napoleon, soon became for the British a war in defence of traditional values, a kind of reactionary crusade against change of any kind. It was therefore very easy to imagine in retrospect that the French revolution was the turning-point in the whole story of reform movements in Britain, that both Pitt and the country he governed turned against reform as soon as its possible consequences became frighteningly obvious across the Channel.

As well as distorting and over-simplifying the facts of history, such a view seriously underrates the political astuteness of William Pitt. He knew well enough that a politician needed to have a reputation for consistency and that he must therefore continue to appear as the champion of those reforming movements he had made use of in his rise to power. He also knew that those movements – and above all the movement for Parliamentary reform – aroused the deepest suspicions of George III. The King was a deeply pious man who felt that it was his solemn duty to preserve intact the constitution which he had at the time of his coronation sworn to maintain. His reluctance to accept the independence of the American colonists was not just a reactionary stubbornness: it sprang from an agonising feeling of dereliction of duty and a consciousness that God might well condemn and even punish him for permitting this erosion of his dominions. He determined to stand out resolutely against any further change in the constitution, especially if that change involved the position of Parliament, whose statutes he had sworn to observe, or the privileges of the Church of England, whose supremacy he had sworn to maintain. It was George III, not the French revolution, that turned Pitt the reformer into Pitt the conservative. And, since Pitt was involved with

George III for almost a decade before he went to war against the French revolution, his fight to preserve his political consistency – and to make reform into a millstone round his opponents' necks rather than his own – was that much more prolonged and that much more difficult. When he confronted the French revolution he had the bulk of the country behind him, but he confronted the King in private and alone. It was during those confrontations that he played and won the game of politics.

Parliamentary reform was soon disposed of. When Pitt's radical friends brought forward a reform motion in 1784 he voted for it but told them that it was 'greatly out of season at this juncture'. So it was, for he was still engaged in the aftermath of the General Election which had confirmed him in power and from which he sought to squeeze every ounce of advantage. It was not very edifying to hear the King's chief minister declaim against the iniquities of the existing electoral system while he was doing his best to exploit those iniquities to the full. At Westminster, for instance, Charles Fox had been returned by a comparatively narrow majority and the defeated candidate demanded a scrutiny of the votes. Pitt used government money and government influence in Parliament to back this demand and even told one of his friends that 'he had no doubt of Fox being thrown out'. By April 1785, when he finally abandoned the attempt, he had spent £9,000 and had seriously discredited his administration. Even Daniel Pulteney, an obedient government supporter, wrote that the ministry's reputation had suffered badly from this 'odious business'. The King, who had had a quarter of a century's experience of the dirty side of British politics, considered that it was better for his ministers to play the existing game, even if they lost as in this case, than to propose new rules: but he was well aware that Pitt had committed himself to reform and must be allowed to make a public gesture towards it. 'Mr Pitt must recollect,' he wrote, 'that though I have thought it unfortunate that he had early engaged himself in this measure, yet that I have ever said that as he was clear of the propriety of the measure, he ought to lay his thoughts before the House.' Pitt did so, introducing a Bill on 18 April 1785 for the voluntary buying up of some thirty small boroughs and the redistribution of the resulting seats among London and the counties. Moderate though it was, the proposal was defeated by 74 votes. It was clear that George III had been right in thinking that Pitt could safely be allowed to make his gesture. Honour was now satisfied. Both the King and the country gentlemen had shown that they had put Pitt in to clear out corrupt Whigs, not to clear out corruption itself. He accepted their verdict and made no further attempt to introduce parliamentary reform.

Meanwhile the Dissenters, members of the various nonconformist congregations which could not bring themselves to subscribe to the tenets of the Church of England, were bent on a much more fundamental measure of reform than the redistribution of a few borough seats. They wanted to get the penal legislation of the previous century repealed, so that they could take a full part in the running of the country, both at a local and at a national level, even though they were not Anglicans. This idea that citizenship should not depend on churchmanship, that the holding of public office and the exercise of political power were part of what the American Declaration of Independence had called man's 'unalienable rights', was much too revolutionary for Pitt's stomach. When his father had declared that he 'rejoiced that America had resisted', back in 1766, he had not meant that America was free to coin revolutionary phrases about natural rights and then infect England with them. He had meant that Americans were praiseworthy as long as they copied the seventeenth-century Englishmen who had humbled the Stuarts. And this depended on holding fast to the Anglican Church, membership of which was the essential prerequisite for the full enjoyment of English liberties. There does not seem to have been any deep spirituality in the Pitt family, either in the father or in the son: for them religion was a civic duty rather than a transcendent experience and they failed to see why those who shirked their duty should be tolerated. When Henry Beaufoy, a follower of Lansdowne – as were so many of the Dissenters' sympathisers – introduced a motion for the repeal of the penal laws in March 1787, Pitt made a coldly hostile speech in which he observed that many Dissenters held violent and dangerous opinions. Some accused the Church of England of being a relic of Popery; some even suggested – horror of horrors – that the country had no need of an Established Church at all. He conceded that there were sensible and moderate Dissenters who did not share these terrifying views, but he saw no way of separating the sheep from the goats. Therefore, he concluded, 'the bulwark must be kept up against all'. The motion was defeated, as were renewed attempts made by the Dissenters in 1789 and 1790.

Fox standing on the hustings before St Paul's Church in Covent Garden in the election of 1784.

St ANNS

Pitt's doughty defence of the Established Church provides a good indication, perhaps the clearest that we can hope for, of his attitude to the reforming movements of his time. During the nineteenth century, when politicians became increasingly idealistic and even came to think that ideals could be made to shape events, there was much discussion of Pitt's apparent inconsistency and of the reasons for it. For some it was a matter of chronology – at a certain point in time the French revolution turned him from a reformer into a conservative and even a reactionary – while for others it was a matter of straightforward duplicity: having used the cry of reform in order to get into power he then dropped it as soon as it became inconvenient. In fact, however, the inconsistencies of William Pitt were less glaring than they have appeared to those moralising historians who were begotten of the Victorian age and seem to have survived, in a surprising number of cases, into the twentieth century. The one issue on which he did change his position, totally and dramatically, was the issue of parliamentary reform. He supported it in the 1780s and he prosecuted men for suggesting it in the 1790s. It must be remembered, however, that the reforms in question were quite different: his own proposals, both in 1783 and in 1785, were aimed principally at confirming and extending the supremacy of the landed class, while those that were being aired a decade later were much more sweeping and could have produced a genuine threat to the existing hierarchy. Pitt believed in an aristocracy and he therefore distinguished between two kinds of change. Change which purified the aristocracy, which recalled it to its duty and made it less corrupt and less cruel and more capable of ruling, constituted reform and should be encouraged and promoted. Change which undermined the aristocracy and questioned its right to rule was revolutionary and destructive and must be firmly resisted.

Unfortunately for Pitt's reputation the causes with which he became involved were to acquire in the succeeding century a new significance and a new dimension. Parliamentary reform, in particular, became associated with social change and with the so-called 'rise of the middle classes'. Pitt himself had little time for the middle classes and they for their part had few illusions about him. Many of them were Dissenters, especially in the newly industrialised areas in the Midlands and around Liverpool, and they saw clearly enough that the 'bulwark' which Pitt wanted to maintain against them was part of the defence works surrounding the squirearchy and the citadel of landed property. One prominent manufacturer from Birmingham complained bitterly in 1785 about the disdain with which the Pitt administration treated deputations from trade and industry; and if the men of money came in the end to trust Pitt as implicitly as the men of land it was largely because of what Joseph Farington once called 'the high idea they have of his financiering talents'. Those talents, like the early interest in parliamentary reform, were taken by some subsequent historians to mean that Pitt was a champion of the middle classes against the languorous and irresponsible aristocrats of the Whig party; and this in turn led to charges of inconsistency and even dishonesty because he later came to champion the social hierarchy against all change. In fact the only enemies he saw were languor and irresponsibility, not this class or that. His metaphor of the bulwark that must be kept up revealed his character and his prejudices as clearly as did the cause in which it was uttered.

Both Pitt and the King were aware, however, that the business of government necessitated the employment of comparatively humble men, men who had their way to make in the world, and that the increasingly professional nature of government office meant that political services could no longer be rewarded by convenient sinecures. Coming on top of Burke's pruning of sinecures in 1782, this meant that the game of politics itself, the constant attention to men's ambitions in order to ensure that they voted the right way in the Commons, was made more difficult. 'While desires increase,' the King wrote to Pitt sadly in January 1787, 'the means of satisfying people have been much diminished.' Pitt's own constituents, the reverend gentlemen of the University of Cambridge, were even more depressed by the paucity of patronage, the apparently decreasing number of bishoprics and deaneries and pleasantly undemanding country livings, which he had to offer. On one occasion when he was to be present at the University Sermon it was suggested that the text should be taken from the sixth chapter of the Gospel according to St John: 'There is a lad here which hath five barley loaves and two small fishes, but what are they among so many?' Neither Pitt nor his royal master doubted for a moment that honourable employment in church and state was the natural birthright of noblemen and gentlemen – even the Patriots at their most enthusiastic had only wanted such offices shared out more fairly, not suppressed altogether – but it was difficult to please everybody. One obvious way out was to offer promotion rather than employment, to dangle marquisates before earls, earldoms before baronets and baronetcies before simple gentlemen. The number of peers created, usually for political services rendered, certainly increased significantly during Pitt's ministry, but there is no evidence to suggest that he devalued the peerage or filled it up with newly enriched members of the middle classes. Pitt himself was well aware of the dangers and he told the Duke of Rutland quite early in his ministry that 'a variety of circumstances has unavoidably led me to recommend a larger addition to the British peerage than I like or than I think quite creditable; and I am on that account very desirous not to increase it now farther than is absolutely necessary'. Not many of the letters he wrote to applicants for peerages have been preserved – perhaps because they were considered too curt – but the letters he received on this score, dozens of which are in the Chatham papers in the Public Record Office, do not suggest that he gave away honours indiscriminately. Requests are repeated time and time again and there are many complaints of neglect, especially from those whose social status is too humble or whose political services are too meagre. It is the correspondence of a man concerned to make aristocrats more businesslike rather than businessmen more aristocratic.

Some of the least businesslike of the aristocrats were those who gathered round the Prince of Wales. While Pitt and the other ministers of the King were too busy to be fashionable, the Prince's friends were too fashionable to allow themselves to be thought busy. Many of them – including Charles Fox, one of the closest and most politically significant of them all – were in fact capable of sustained hard work, but they did not care for the fact to be known. While the King was gaining the affection of his people because of a respectability that verged on sheer dullness, the Prince was regarded with a mixture of fascination and disgust because of his extravagance and frivolity. He and his friends seemed to dance and lounge and gamble their way through life, running up enormous debts and presumably indulging in exotic vices which the public and the caricaturists guessed at with delighted lubricity. In fact the Prince's private life was even more bizarre than the public thought: he fell in love with Maria Fitzherbert, a lady several years older than himself who was not only twice widowed and of humble birth but was also a Roman Catholic, which meant that he could not

OPPOSITE A Rowlandson cartoon entitled 'Exhibition Stare Case' on the activities of the Prince of Wales and his friends.

DISCRIPTIVE

Maria Fitzherbert who was secretly married to the Prince of Wales in 1785.

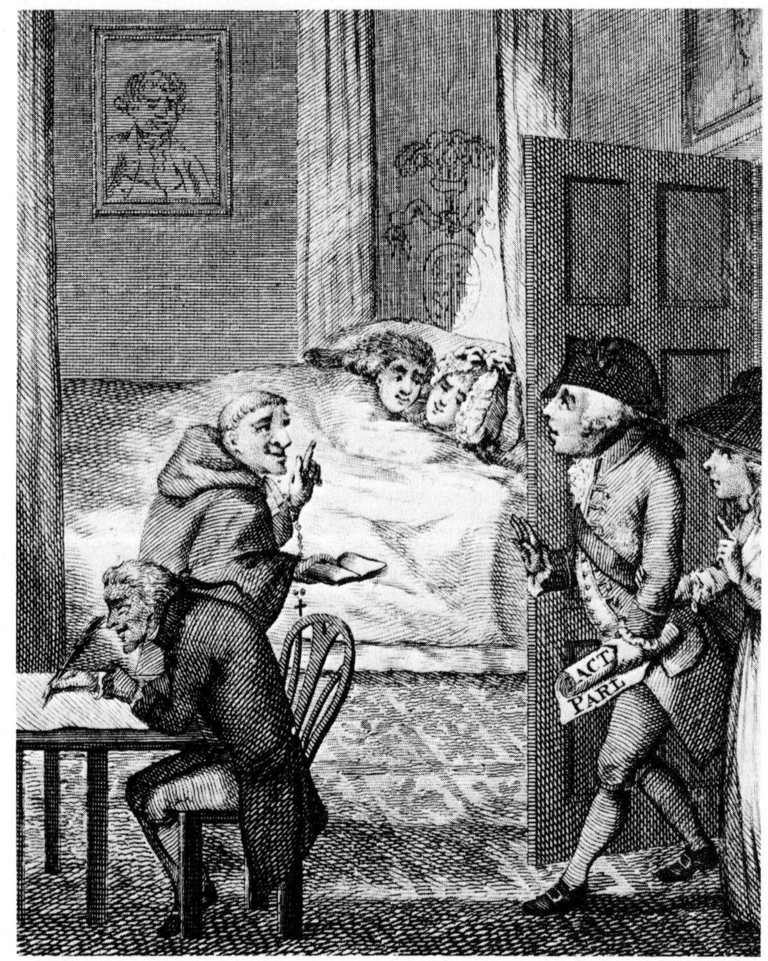

George III enters his son's room with a document forbidding the marriage of royal princes without his consent. On the wall is a portrait of Fox who had believed the Prince when he denied the marriage.

marry her unless he renounced the throne. She refused to be his mistress and at first she also rejected any idea of a secret marriage, even though the Prince resorted to tears and tantrums and all manner of histrionics. Finally he gave himself a minor stab wound and arranged for her to be brought to his bedside to see him ashen and bloodstained, hovering on the very brink of the untimely death to which she had driven him. At first Maria broke down under this treatment and agreed to marry him; but when she recovered her wits and realised that she had been the victim of a grotesque charade she fled abroad. In the end, however, the couple were married in December 1785 – secretly, because the Prince could not marry without the King's consent, even if he had been prepared to renounce the throne. In the spring of 1787, when the opposition leaders brought up the Prince's affairs in the House of Commons and demanded that his very considerable debts should be paid by Parliament, there were open references to the rumours of a secret marriage. Fox denied these vehemently, as he had not been let in on the secret and genuinely believed that the marriage had not taken place. Then, to his horror, he discovered that the Prince had lied to him and that he had been tricked into making a false statement in the Commons – a statement which an indignant Mrs Fitzherbert now insisted should be withdrawn. The Prince's affairs were no longer a mere sorry absurdity: they had become the subject of a major political crisis.

On the face of things it was a superb opportunity for Pitt to make political capital. The opposition was divided and dismayed, furious with its leaders and uncertain what to believe. Pitt had only to stand firm, refusing payment of the debts until the Prince revealed the reason for their sudden increase – which was, of course, the allowance he was paying Mrs Fitzherbert. Then, surely, Pitt's opponents would be totally discredited and his own position secured. But Pitt had been in the political game long enough to know that the really powerful pieces in it, the pieces that wore crowns and coronets, could not be manipulated with the same nonchalance as the minor pieces. Reformers and businessmen, with their lofty principles and their sordid calculations, might form the subject of political action but kings and princes controlled its object, which was power. Power today depended on the reigning monarch, power tomorrow might well depend on his son and heir. Fox, who seemed assured of power in the future, could not bring himself to give up the present: he still hoped against hope that George III could be persuaded to employ him again. Similarly Pitt, in full enjoyment of the present, still had hopes for the future, hopes that the Prince of Wales when he succeeded might see the advantage of continuing him in office. Both men therefore tried to moderate the quarrel between the royal father and son. Pitt waited dutifully on the Prince, taking his commands and transmitting to him, as tactfully and respectfully as he could, those of the King. George III told Pitt repeatedly how much he valued his skill and discretion in this delicate matter, but the Prince was less appreciative. He blamed everybody but himself for the difficulties he had created and he insisted on believing that Pitt was deliberately making matters worse. In the end there was a grudging reconciliation between King and Prince, a compromise settlement of the debt question and a tacit acceptance of Mrs Fitzherbert's position. The scandal gradually grew cold. Unhappily for Pitt, his relations with the Prince grew colder still.

In this tense situation the key factor was the health of the King. He was approaching his fiftieth birthday and there were those about the Court who detected signs of old age in him and spoke of the next reign as being just around the corner. Some remembered his mysterious illness in 1765, which had been officially dismissed as a bad cold but had nevertheless led him while still in his twenties to make detailed provisions for his own death and for the minority of his son. Now, in the summer of 1788, there was a recurrence of the symptoms of 1765 and there were fears, as there had been then, that the King's afflictions were mental as well as physical. It now seems fairly certain that he suffered throughout his life from porphyria, a metabolic disorder whose causes and nature were unknown in the eighteenth century. Its effects on him were appalling, sufficiently so to explain his mental breakdown and his eventual retreat into prolonged senility. In 1788-9, however, he was strong enough to throw off the attack and recover the balance of his mind and the use of his body. The crisis of his illness came in November 1788, when he lapsed into delirium and terrified the dinner-table at Windsor by foaming at the mouth and rushing at the Prince of Wales. For many weeks it seemed as though he would either die or remain permanently insane. In the end, however, his remarkably robust constitution triumphed both over the disease and over the treatment he was given, which can only be described as diabolical – a succession of emetics, purgatives, blisterings and periods of confinement in a strait-waistcoat. His mental state was aggravated rather than alleviated and its physical causes were almost entirely ignored. Nevertheless, the King recovered. By the end of February 1789 he was sufficiently composed to deal with public business again and on 23 April, St George's Day, there was an official service of thanksgiving in St Paul's Cathedral for his return to health.

During those critical months, while the King lay trussed in a strait-waistcoat or sat strapped into Dr Willis's 'restraining chair', the politicians wrestled with one another on the edge of a crumbling precipice of uncertainty. Nobody could be sure whether Pitt would be hurled from office as a result of the King's death or prolonged insanity or whether Fox would be finally damned in the event of a royal recovery. At Windsor, where he took charge of things, the Prince of Wales showed genuine distress at his father's pitiful condition; but in London, where his friends in the opposition asserted his hereditary right to assume the powers of a Regent forthwith, he showed unrelenting hostility towards his father's ministers and especially towards Pitt. Pitt played for time, insisting that a Regency could only be set up by Act of Parliament. His Regency Bill was ingenious, dividing power between the Prince and the Queen and preventing the Prince from doing things which his father would not be able to undo in the event of his recovery. His tactics were also ingenious: he smoked out the false friends in his own ministry – notably Thurlow, the Lord Chancellor – and he put Fox into a position where he had to defend the prerogatives and hereditary rights of the Prince of Wales against the claims of Parliament. But in the end it was the physical resilience of George III, not the mental resource of William Pitt, that decided the political future of the country. If the King's illness had lasted a few days longer the Regency Bill would have passed, the Prince would have become Regent and an administration led by Fox would have been appointed. If these things had once been done they would have been extremely hard to undo, for all Pitt's provisions and conditions. George III said after his recovery, when he read the accounts of what had been done during his illness, that if his Parliament had once branded him as a lunatic by passing the Regency Bill he would have retired to Hanover and 'no power on earth should have prevailed on him to resume the government'. For all its ingenuity Pitt's Bill had offended the King it was intended to protect as well as the Prince it was intended to restrain.

OVERLEAF
The thanksgiving service at St Paul's Cathedral on the king's recovery.

Dec 1788.

Prince Pitt!

O R,

The Miniſter of the Crown

GREATER THAN THE

Heir Apparent!

" *I Affirm that the Prince of Wales has*
" *no more* RIGHT *to be Regent*,
" THAN ANY OTHER SUBJECT!"
-----Mr. Pitt's Speech on Wedneſday.

That is to ſay, NO MORE RIGHT THAN

William Pitt!

Who, having already deſtroyed the People's Rights by an undue Exertion of the Prerogative of the Crown, is now willing to raiſe himſelf above that Prerogative, by *ſeizing on the Sovereignty of theſe Kingdoms*.

A pamphlet decrying Pitt's opposition to the Regency of the Prince of Wales.

The crisis left an indelible mark on William Pitt. It showed him once and for all the real nature of the political game and of the power which was its ultimate objective. In theory the King's chief minister exercised power in accordance with the wishes of Parliament, but in practice he held it by favour of royal personages, be they Kings or Regents. The King had given and the King could take away. Worse still, the King could now blackmail his ministers by threatening to fall ill again if they tried to push him into things which were against his inclinations or his conscience. When Pitt pressed him, some weeks after his recovery, to agree to an army promotion for a nephew of the Marquis of Buckingham, the King replied: 'To say the truth, though I am recovering, my mind is not strong enough as yet to stand little ruffles, and still more so when they relate to Lord Buckingham, who does not stand well in my mind.' In this case Pitt got his way; but as time went on the King became more obdurate, particularly over things which seemed to go against his coronation oath and therefore to involve the risk of further divine punishment of the kind he had just suffered. The nature of British politics did indeed undergo a change in the 1790s, with the result that Pitt appeared more and more as a conservative, as the defender of the authority of kings rather than of the rights of peoples; but this was not simply the result of the French revolution or of the British reaction to it. It was also the result of the knife-edge on which Pitt's power rested and the King's exploitation, conscious or unconscious, of his minister's precarious position.

Meanwhile it was the opposition politicians who were placed in 1789 in the unenviable position of men who had tried to climb to power over the body of a King who now turned out not to be dead after all. Some of them refused to believe in the recovery and told one another that George III was in reality a hopeless lunatic who was being propped up and made to appear sane by Pitt and the Queen and their fellow-conspirators. Nonsense of this sort made little headway and by the end of the year, after the King had made a tour of the West country amid scenes of wild enthusiasm and loyal acclaim, Fox and his party were widely regarded as the seditious and heartless enemies of a wise and popular King. Burke, who had said some particularly indiscreet things about George III having been hurled from his throne by God Almighty, was pilloried mercilessly in the press as a half-crazed fanatic and a would-be regicide. In 1790, when he first came out as a bitter critic of the French revolution,

Burke drew upon himself some violent denunciations of his inconsistency – not only of the gulf between his earlier liberal opinions and his present conservatism, but of the sharp contrast between his elaborate concern for the King and Queen of France and his callous contempt for the King and Queen of Great Britain. The divisions which took place within the opposition, culminating in the dramatic breach between Fox and Burke in the spring of 1791, sprang from recriminations over the Regency crisis as well as from differences over the French revolution. And in the summer of 1792, when events in France made the leaders of the English aristocracy think that the time had come for a government of national unity, they based their calculations on the possibility of the Prince's accession as much as on the possibility of war with France. Lord Malmesbury noted in his diary, after a conversation with the Whig leader Portland, that they had agreed that a coalition with Pitt was advisable because 'Pitt was of such consequence in the country, and the Prince of Wales so little respected, that we considered it as impossible for him to form an administration of which Pitt was not to be a part; that an attempt to the contrary, in the present temper of people's minds, would produce the greatest confusion, and even go to endanger the succession'. The negotiations of 1792 failed, but in 1794 the bulk of the Whig party, under the Duke of Portland himself, joined Pitt's ministry. Only Fox and a small body of his friends continued in opposition. They found it so dispiriting that in the spring of 1797 many of them, including Fox himself, gave up attending Parliament. Pitt had come nearer to complete victory in the political game than any other minister of the century, but he had not done so because of a British crusade in defence of the monarchy of France. He had done so because even his opponents now considered him indispensable to the monarchs of Britain, future as well as present.

6

THE HAND OF WAR

One thing which foreign visitors to England in the eighteenth century almost always noticed was the absence of the signs and traces of war. Ancient towns had let their defensive walls fall into disrepair and less ancient ones did not even have any. There were few soldiers to be seen in the streets and there were none of the great barracks and parade grounds and military establishments so common on the continent of Europe. Even in Ireland and Scotland, where there were still signs of military occupation by English troops, there was little that indicated any great fear of foreign invasion. Great Britain did indeed seem to be a fortress built by nature against infection and the hand of war. And Chatham, who had been as proud as any man of this immunity from the hand of war and the power of standing armies, had been able to give his fellow-countrymen the final and most piquant satisfaction of all: the chance to profit from foreign war and revel in glorious victories without any fear of military domination at home. As long ago as the 1730s he and his Patriot friends had promised that they could humble Britain's enemies by means of colonial warfare and sea warfare only, without the need to raise enormous armies and risk involvement in Europe. The wars that had followed had in fact only partially redeemed that promise and they had led in the end to the humiliation of American independence; but in retrospect the failures and disappointments were forgotten and the splendid dream of Patriot war and colonial conquest, the glory of the Pitt family, retained much of its appeal.

For William Pitt the younger the dream became a nightmare. Much as he valued peace and the financial stability which peace made possible, he was always conscious of the martial aspect of his Patriot inheritance and he was not the man to neglect a chance to continue his father's work and humble the colonial power of France. By the beginning of 1793 it seemed that such a chance had come: France was torn apart by revolution and civil war and she was facing invasion by a coalition of European powers. Yet the war upon which Pitt embarked in that year, far from producing easy colonial conquests and renewed Patriot glory, produced instead sufferings and humiliations and continental involvements upon an unprecedented scale. It undid all his earlier achievements and by the end of the century he himself spoke of 'evils and growing dangers of which I see no adequate remedy'. In the end it killed him, piling upon his shoulders a load of anxiety and overwork and tension under which his health finally broke down.

PREVIOUS PAGE Pitt in his uniform as Colonel Commandant of the Cinque Ports Volunteers. Walmer Castle is in the background.

A smug British view of the contrast between Britain and France.

The English, who tend to see themselves and their statesmen as essentially peaceable people, have produced their own heroic version of William Pitt's tragedy. For them the poignant contrast between the relaxed confidence of his early years and the desperate sadness of his end is seen as the product of a duty unflinchingly done, a mission faithfully completed. They take at its face value his famous speech in November 1805, when he said that 'England has saved herself by her exertions and will, as I trust, save Europe by her example'. They see Pitt as the man who gave his life – and, incidentally, the lives of many of his countrymen – in order to save Europe and the world from the ugly pattern of anarchy and tyranny which emerged from the cataclysm of the French revolution. Europe, on the other hand, has been a little reluctant to recognise William Pitt as her saviour. The English legend of Pitt's heroism is elbowed aside in European history books by the rather different legend of 'Pitt's gold', the picture which the French revolutionary propagandists drew of the British prime minister pouring out bribes and secret subsidies in order to stir up the enemies of France and subvert her government. Somewhere between these two extremes lies the truth, difficult to find but more worthy of pursuit than the legends.

The chief obstacle in the pursuit of this particular truth has always been the notion that the French revolution which began in the year 1789 was a change so total and so apocalyptic that it shattered the diplomatic pattern of Europe and forced all France's neighbours, Britain included, to stand their existing foreign policies on their heads. This has led to the idea that Pitt's policy was one of peace and goodwill towards the France of the *ancien régime*, succeeded by one of suspicion and finally of open hostility towards revolutionary France. In fact Pitt understood perfectly clearly, from the moment he took over the management of the King's government, that France was Britain's most dangerous enemy and that her appetite for revenge had by no means been satisfied by her apparent victory in the War of American Independence. The earliest of all his tasks as prime minister, the drafting of an alternative to Fox's India Bill, was overshadowed by the fear that by the time it came into force there might be no British India to administer. 'We shall lose the East Indies, for Holland and France are united to ruin our trade and in order to drive us out of the East Indies', wrote one British diplomat in February 1784, while Pitt was struggling to keep the first version of his own India Bill alive in the House of Commons. Nor was it only a matter of India itself: the means of getting there was also liable to lead to war between the two countries. There was violent Anglo-French rivalry in the Near East, where a French agent was negotiating with the Egyptians to get control of the isthmus of Suez, already seen as the key to the control of India and as the site of a future canal from the Mediterranean into the Red Sea. And in Ireland the French seemed even more dangerous, stirring up discontent on England's very doorstep. By August of 1784 Pitt was receiving reports of secret meetings at which French agents presided while Irishmen knelt to drink the health of the King of France.

Worst of all, the French were intriguing against British influence in the Dutch Republic. 'The people of Amsterdam repent having trusted to the friendship and support of France,' wrote one of Pitt's colleagues in October 1784, 'I believe our late fellow-subjects in America have as little to boast of the sincerity of the French as the Dutch have.' His optimism was premature: the financial and commercial links which had enabled France to bring the Dutch into the American war on their side were by no means broken and during the first few years of Pitt's administration the French Foreign Office steadily strengthened the anti-British party in Holland, the most important of the seven United Provinces which went to make up the Dutch Republic. As well as having a dynastic interest in the United Provinces – the Stadtholder, nearest equivalent to a king in the Dutch constitution, was a cousin of George III – the British had a vitally important financial interest. A large proportion of British government stock was in Dutch hands and the money market of Amsterdam underpinned with its enormous credit resources many of the operations of the City of London. A struggle therefore developed which concerned 'Pitt's gold' in more senses than one: he was sending gold to the United Provinces, secret subsidies as well as official aid, in order to stave off a revolution there which might jeopardise the credit structure with which Britain's own currency was closely linked. In the summer of 1787 it seemed as though the French were about to win the game and overthrow the Stadtholder, but skilful manoeuvring on the part of British agents, together with military intervention by the Prussians, succeeded in crushing the pro-French party and demolishing France's whole position in the United Provinces. In 1788 this victory was followed up with a Triple Alliance of Great Britain, Prussia and the Dutch Republic – a powerful combination which was clearly directed primarily against France.

In England this victory was celebrated with an enthusiasm which was extremely flattering to Pitt. Almost every member of the House of Commons joined to pay him tribute and shower congratulations upon him. Officially the Foreign Secretary was the Marquis of Carmarthen, later created Duke of Leeds; but nobody seriously imagined that the son of the great Chatham would allow vital questions of peace and war and foreign relations to be decided by anyone but himself. In this the popular belief was correct and the popular enthusiasm was properly directed: Pitt had assumed overall control of operations in the United Provinces and he was to interfere increasingly in foreign affairs over the next few years until in 1791 he drove Leeds to resign. The triumph over the French in 1787 gave Pitt new confidence and made him realise, as his father had realised long before, that in terms of popularity and political standing one successful display of belligerence to a foreign foe – especially to France – was worth a score of ingenious administrative measures. Some months before, when the Commercial

Although Pitt had a home in Kent, he could spare little time for it and spent most of his life in London.

RIGHT 'The Old Swan' at Bayswater in 1790.
BELOW Kensington Palace in 1794.

RIGHT Mansion House from Poultry, 1798.

LEFT St Paul's Cathedral behind Blackfriars Bridge, 1797.

Treaty with France was being debated in the Commons, he had rebuked Fox in the loftiest terms for speaking of France as 'the unalterable enemy of England'; but even at that time Pitt had known perfectly well that the Treaty was the product of mutual distrust as well as of common interest. The negotiations which led to it had been anything but friendly and the French government had been warned by its chief commercial adviser that Pitt was acting 'neither through magnanimity nor a liking for France'. By the time the Treaty actually came into operation, in May 1787, the vestiges of magnanimity were even more difficult to find and by November, when the victory in the United Provinces was celebrated in the Commons, they had almost totally disappeared. From then onwards Pitt's attitude to France smacked more of his father's watchful opportunism than of any readiness to crusade for kings against revolutionaries.

Meanwhile in France there was increasing hatred of the British in general and of Pitt in particular. French industry was unable to compete with the cheap British manufactured goods that came flooding into the country under the terms of the Commercial Treaty, so that there was large-scale unemployment and an industrial depression which soon spread to the countryside as well. At the same time there were ugly rumours, not by any means without foundation, that the French King's ministers were being manipulated by international financial speculators. In fact these speculators had no connection with Pitt: most of them were based either in Geneva or in Brussels and their intervention in French internal affairs was aimed at safeguarding the very large sums they had invested in French government stock. But it did not take much to connect the Treaty with the speculators and thus to propagate the legend that the French government itself was a mere puppet of the sinister British businessmen who were out to ruin France. Even before he appeared in the autumn of 1787 as the victor in the struggle for the Amsterdam money market, Pitt was coming to be seen in France as the bloated spider at the centre of a web of international intrigue and subversion. The legend of 'Pitt's gold' had been born.

By November 1787 there was a general feeling throughout France that war with England was inevitable. English travellers were horrified by the vehemence of the outcry against their country, while in Paris the secretary of the British embassy told his government that 'the ministers have no longer any confidence in what is said to them on the part of England'. As if conscious of Pitt's apparently bellicose intentions, he went on to point out 'with the utmost deference' that it would be wiser to leave France to dissolve into civil strife than to provoke her into war and thus give her a chance to regain her national unity and stability. In fact neither Pitt nor George III wanted war at this stage, though the latter was insistent that the defence estimates should not be reduced and that France should know that 'after what has passed we think it right everywhere without any hostile intention to be guarded against an unexpected attack'. The British government tried to remain aloof from the internal troubles of France, but it was not always easy. The Duke of Orleans, an acknowledged leader of the opposition to his cousin the King of France, was also a crony of the Prince of Wales and paid frequent visits to England. One of Pitt's informants wrote in 1786 that Orleans and his entourage 'keep up the wild spirits of His Royal Highness and indeed I am almost led to suppose that there may be some design in their apparently idle visit to this kingdom'. Two years later, when the Prince seemed about to come to power as the result of his father's illness, it seemed as though there might have been some ground for these suspicions. Orleans and his party sent their congratulations to the Prince of Wales and assumed that as Regent he would send Pitt packing and give his support to the revolutionary movement which was gathering momentum in France.

While French gossip writers made the most of this supposed link between opposition to Louis XVI and opposition to George III – they were still talking of the Prince of Wales as leader of an English revolution as late as November 1792 – the English for their part singled out Orleans as the prime mover of events in France. In July and August of 1789, when news came through of the fall of the Bastille and the French King's surrender to the newly proclaimed National Assembly, it was Orleans who appeared in popular prints in London as the hero who had brought freedom to France. Later, when British attitudes to the revolution changed, he figured as a sinister conspirator stirring up the mob in order to topple his cousin from the throne.

Pitt's own involvement in the French revolution began early in July 1789 when the French government, rightly seeing the high price of bread as one of the basic causes of unrest, sent an urgent request to England for permission to buy grain.

The fall of the Bastille in 1789.

Normally the export of grain from England was only allowed when the price was low, which it was not at that time since there had been poor harvests in England as in France. Instead of authorising the export himself Pitt put the request before the House of Commons, which turned it down. When the French managed to import a few thousand sacks of grain from Shoreham in Sussex by pushing down the price artificially, it was Pitt who personally promised the House that he would do everything in his power to make sure that the perpetrators of the fraud were punished. In the course of the next few months the so-called 'conspiracy' to keep France short of grain became the subject of bitter recriminations in Paris, so that by the end of the year Pitt had become doubly a villain in French eyes, subsidising agitators with one hand and callously withholding food supplies with the other.

Meanwhile the Duke of Orleans had appeared in England yet again, this time with proposals for the British and French governments to take joint action in the Austrian Netherlands –

present-day Belgium – where there had also been a revolution that year. There was talk of inviting the Prince of Wales to put himself at the head of the Belgian revolution, a suggestion which horrified even those opposition politicians who had supported Orleans and the French revolution up to this time. George III was furious and told his ministers that he would have nothing to do with the idea. Belgium, as Pitt well knew, was vital in British foreign policy. Even the Patriots, with all their emphasis on colonial warfare and their rejection of European involvement, could not ignore the fact that Belgium held the key to British security and to British trade. Quite apart from the long-standing fear of France swallowing up the whole of the Netherlands and thus controlling the opposite coast of the English Channel, there was the specific question of the river Scheldt. Antwerp, once one of Europe's greatest ports, had been idle for more than a hundred years because it stood on the Scheldt above the point at which that river was crossed by the border between Belgium and the Dutch Republic. The Dutch feared that their economy in general, and the port of Amsterdam in particular, would suffer from the competition which would result if the Scheldt were reopened and Antwerp's trade revived. There had been an international crisis in 1784 when the Austrians had tried to reopen the Scheldt. It had been clear then, and it remained clear now, that any further attempt to reopen the river to trade would probably involve Great Britain in war. It was all very well for Pitt to tell his mother, as he did in July 1789, that France was now 'an object of compassion, even to a rival'; but it was clear that the compassion was tinged with suspicion and distrust. It was also accompanied by a growing realisation that if the other powers of Europe would deal with France's armies then the comparative weakness of her naval and colonial position could be turned to Britain's advantage.

The impact of the French revolution on British politics became clear early in 1790 when the defence estimates came up for debate in the Commons. The opposition took the chance to attack the government on the grounds that there was no longer any need for such high defence expenditure now that French absolutism, the traditional danger against which free-born Britons had had to arm themselves, was at an end. Fox, in particular, retracted his earlier view that the British and the French were 'unalterable enemies' and proclaimed that France now stood for universal brotherhood and not universal tyranny. It was then that Burke first produced in public his own very different appraisal of the French revolution as a movement which threatened to engulf the whole of Europe in a new tyranny more sinister than anything the French monarchy had devised. Pitt smoothed the quarrel over and concluded the debate 'with becoming gravity and dignity and a reserve on both sides of the question, as related to France, fit for a person in a ministerial station'. But for all his apparent reserve he can hardly have been unaware, even at that early stage, of the advantages which this split within the opposition promised to give him. The quarrel between Fox and Burke, feeding on the bitterness which already existed as a result of the Regency crisis and the growing burden of the Hastings impeachment, eventually erupted in April 1791. After an angry scene in the Commons Burke broke off all relations with Fox; and three years later the great majority of the Whig party, with Burke's approval, joined Pitt's government on Pitt's terms. Fox was left to lead a dwindling minority and to oppose as best he could the increasingly repressive nature of the Pitt administration.

Meanwhile Pitt was putting to good use the military preparedness which Burke applauded and Fox deplored. The Spaniards, claiming that their possession of the west coast of North America extended right up into Canada, had attacked and seized a British settlement at Nootka Sound near Vancouver. If Spanish claims to northward expansion from California were a little shaky, British claims to westward expansion from Quebec were even shakier; but considerations of this sort did not have much influence on British public opinion, which burst into a frenzy of anti-Spanish jingoism. There were reminders of Chatham's early days, when he had helped to push the government into war in order to avenge a British sea captain who had had his ear cut off by Spanish coastguards. There were also reminders, closer and more uncomfortable, of Fox's success in unseating Shelburne in 1783 when he had made unpopular concessions to the colonial pretensions of Spain and France. Now Fox adopted the same tactics, forgetting his earlier arguments against defence and demanding the most vigorous action against Spain. Pitt took personal charge of the affair from the beginning: he saw how politically charged it was and he did not want to risk defeat in the General Election which was almost due and which in fact he called in the summer of 1790. By the time the old Parliament was dissolved in June of that year the worst of the crisis was

OPPOSITE Pitt seated at his desk in 1801, drawn by H. Eldridge.

over: Spain had appealed to France for help and had been told that Louis XVI could do nothing without the approval of the National Assembly, which was not forthcoming. The Spaniards gave in, the General Election was won and a new brand of ruthless British imperialism was born. When the new Parliament met there were congratulations which outdid those of 1787 and then, half way through December, there came the highest honour of all: the offer from the King of the Order of the Garter. The twenty-five Knights of the Garter represented the noblest and most distinguished in the land: even Chatham in all his glory had not been arrayed like one of these.

The offer was not accepted. Pitt knew well enough the nature of his inheritance: the power was his but the glory belonged to the family. He begged the King to bestow the Garter instead on his elder brother John who had inherited the earldom of Chatham. George III agreed, observing that 'this public testimony of approbation will be understood as meant to the whole family'. Pitt's colleagues on the other hand, were not so sure that the royal approbation had been justly earned. Having swept the matter out of their hands, and especially out of the hands of the Foreign Secretary, Pitt had hesitated at the crucial moment and had shown signs of weakness which, in the opinion of some members of the cabinet, might have enabled the Spaniards to spin the affair out until they had secured an American or even a Russian alliance. He had recovered his nerve in July, after the French rebuff to Spain, and had then brought the whole business to a triumphant conclusion. But the seeds of doubt and disunity had been sown. In matters of finance and administration his command over the cabinet was absolute, his supremacy unchallenged. But in matters of war and diplomacy it was very different. Here, in the very sphere in which he most wanted to emulate his father, he was least able to do so. It was perhaps appropriate that the Garter should be bestowed on the earldom of Chatham rather than on the person of William Pitt.

Within a matter of months the doubts were out in the open. It was common knowledge that the cabinet was bitterly divided over Pitt's next venture in foreign policy, the attempt to make Russia give back the territories she had conquered from Turkey on the shores of the Black Sea. In retrospect historians have acclaimed Pitt as the first statesman to see the form which the 'Eastern Question' was to take during the nineteenth century; but at the time he seemed more like a gambler pushing his luck than a prophet of the future. While some opposition speakers condemned him for taking the side of the infidel Turks against a Christian nation, others derided the spectacle of 'the offspring of the immortal Chatham intriguing in all the courts of Europe and setting himself up as the great posture master of the balance of power'. The Duke of Leeds, still smarting from the humiliations of the Nootka Sound affair, insisted that this time he should have the authority as well as the responsibilities of the Foreign Secretary. At first Pitt supported him and even encouraged him in his firm stand against the Russians; but when things became difficult there was a climb-down and a cabinet crisis. Pitt drafted conciliatory dispatches to the Russians, Leeds resigned in protest and the opposition openly rejoiced over the total discomfiture of the administration. Rumour had it that the King was so disgusted by the whole affair that he was prepared to exchange Pitt for Fox; and even Pitt himself admitted that if he had persisted in his policy the government would probably have fallen. He had seriously underestimated the difficulty of getting Parliament's support for war against Russia. Worse still, he had underestimated even more seriously the difficulty of getting his cherished Triple Alliance to act in Eastern Europe with the same unanimity it showed in the West. His father had made the same mistake before him: he had imagined in 1766 that a temporary and partial identity of interests between Britain and Prussia could be the basis of an alliance system that would control the balance of power in Europe. His alliance system had crumbled as a result. Now it seemed that the achievements of his son were sharing the same fate. Appropriately enough it was to Joseph Ewart, his plenipotentiary at the Prussian court, that Pitt confessed with tears in his eyes that the episode had been 'the greatest mortification he had ever experienced'.

Far more serious than the apparent disintegration of the Triple Alliance was the apparent disintegration of the country against which it had been aimed – France. In June 1791, within a few weeks of Pitt's surrender to the Russians, Louis XVI of France attempted to escape from the control of the National Assembly. He and his family left the palace at night in disguise with the intention of joining a force of loyalist troops in eastern France who were ready to defy the Assembly and the revolutionary government in his name. But he was stopped and led back to Paris. The pretence of co-operation between King and Assembly was rescued, but to little avail. Louis's attempted flight had sounded the death-knell of constitutional monarchy in France. To most observers it seemed that his country was now on the brink of civil war, a war which must end either in the establishment of a violently anti-royalist republican regime or in the restoration of the monarchy by means of armed intervention from outside. There were those outside who were ready and waiting: Louis's two younger brothers, the Comte de Provence and the Comte d'Artois, had gathered a large force at Coblentz, just across the frontier in Germany. It included exiled noblemen and other French royalists, as well as an inevitable retinue of spies and adventurers and double agents. It also included a young Swedish nobleman, the Comte de Fersen, who was reputedly the lover of the Queen of France and who had taken a major part in planning the escape attempt. Like many others he saw that the key factor in the whole situation, the thing which would decide the fate of France and the future balance of power in Europe, was the attitude of Great Britain. 'We must know,' he wrote in his diary, 'if that power regards the continuation of anarchy in France as more advantageous than order.'

It was a question that was by no means as simple as it looked. For the rabid enemies of revolution, notably for Burke, the thing was quite straightforward: the French revolution was like an outbreak of deadly and contagious disease which must be eliminated before it infected France's neighbours. Long before Louis XVI's flight Burke had said that armed intervention was the only answer; and now he sent his only son to Coblentz as a kind of envoy extraordinary, at the same time approaching Pitt's government with requests that it should recognise the Coblentz exiles and prepare to go to their aid. Pitt steadily refused to do anything of the kind. He realised that Provence and Artois were probably more concerned to displace their brother than to restore him. He also realised that the Prussians and the Austrians and all the other lesser powers were anxious to despoil France herself and not just the French revolution. The territories they annexed would be claimed as rewards for services rendered rather than as the fruits of conquest, but the result would be the same. This was not just an international crusade against revolution: it was also a continuation in new form of the old balance of power game. And Pitt had just had a sharp reminder of the complexities and pitfalls which were involved in that particular exercise. And so, while the whole of Europe waited to see what Pitt would do, Pitt did nothing.

Burke was furious. When Pitt tried to soothe him by telling him that his fears of an English revolution were exaggerated and that things would go on as they were until the Day of Judgment, Burke replied sharply that it was the day of no judgment that he was afraid of. The remark was unfair, since Pitt's inaction was based not on lack of judgment but on a careful and on the whole accurate assessment of the situation. The Austrians tried to pin him down by putting out a declaration saying in effect that they would act against the French revolution if he would do the same. When he still refused to move they subsided again: they had no wish to quarrel with France on their own. Then, in March 1792, the shrewd and cautious Emperor Leopold of Austria died and was succeeded by a young man of twenty-four eager for military glory. Six weeks later Austria and France were at war and very soon it became clear that the extremists in France, and particularly in Paris, did not trust Louis XVI and his aristocratic officer class to wage the war for them. The Assembly decreed the setting up of a camp near Paris at which a revolutionary army was to be recruited and trained; and in August it was decreed that henceforth the distinction between soldier and civilian no longer existed. France was now not a nation with an army but a nation in arms. And on 10 August 1792 the arms of the nation were turned against its King: the palace of the Tuileries was invaded and the monarchy overthrown. In September the new revolutionary army startled the world by defeating its highly trained professional opponents at the battle of Valmy, while the citizens of Paris horrified the world by murdering more than a thousand helpless prisoners because of a rumour that the royalists were about to organise a prison uprising against the revolution. Finally, on 19 November 1792, the National Convention set up to give France a republican constitution officially offered 'brotherhood and assistance' to revolutionary movements throughout the world. It had taken just seven months for the war of intervention to turn France from a constitutional monarchy into an anti-monarchical regime of unparalleled ferocity.

George III was horrified by the course of events in France and he shared Burke's view that the principles of the French revolution must on no account be allowed to spread to England, let alone to Scotland and Ireland where there were long-standing discontents to be exploited. He was delighted when Pitt told Parliament in the spring of 1792 that any further attempt at electoral reform might produce 'anarchy and confusion'. These sentiments, he told Pitt approvingly, 'must endear him to all lovers of good order and our excellent constitution'. When some of the opposition leaders formed a society called 'The Friends of the People' to press for reform, the King called it a 'daring outrage'; and at the end of May he issued a Royal Proclamation against 'divers wicked and seditious writings'. All this did not mean, however, that he was straining to join in the war of intervention. Even after the decree of 19 November, although he readily agreed to increased military preparations, he still took some time to be converted to the need for war. It was not until January 1793 that he confessed that it might be 'the most desirable conclusion of the present crisis'; and on 2 February, when in fact a French declaration of war

The execution of Louis XVI in La Place de la Révolution.

against Great Britain had already been made, he was still writing that his 'natural sentiments were strong for peace' even though 'duty as well as interest calls on us to join against the most savage as well as unprincipled nation'.

The previous day Pitt had stated in the House of Commons his own position on the great issue of peace or war with the French revolution. He had described the decree of 19 November as 'a direct attack on every government in Europe' and he had declared that the death of Louis XVI on the guillotine – news of which had come through a few days before – meant that 'the dreadful sentence which they have executed on their own unfortunate monarch applies to every sovereign now existing'. But the core of his speech, the part where he moved from

The Duke of York leads the attack upon the French at Valenciennes, 1793.

rhetorical attacks to specific declarations of policy, concerned something less dramatic, something which affected the money market of London rather than monarchies of the world. For the triumphant revolutionary armies had by this time swept into Belgium and had reopened the river Scheldt. Not content with setting aside their monarchy, the French had set aside the victory Pitt had won over that monarchy five years before. Moreover, they had announced their intention of setting aside all the treaties which the monarchy had made. It was for this reason, rather than for Burke's reasons, that Pitt had decided that the French revolution threatened British interests – not because the principles of the French monarchy must be held sacred in order to preserve British stability but because its word must be held sacred to preserve British security:

France can have no right to annul the stipulations relative to the Scheldt, unless she has also the right to set aside equally all the other treaties between all the powers of Europe, and all the other rights of England or of her allies. England will never consent that France shall arrogate the power of annulling at her pleasure, and under the pretence of a natural right of which she makes herself the only judge, the political system of Europe established by solemn treaties and guaranteed by the consent of all the powers.

For the next five years Pitt's conduct of the war was based on the order of priorities reflected in that speech and on the traditional aims of Great Britain in any war with France. For at least a century French privateers based on Dunkirk had endangered British shipping in time of war; and so Pitt insisted that the Belgian campaign of 1793 should include an attack on Dunkirk. At the opening of the campaign Austrian successes, together with treachery within the French army itself, seemed to promise an early reconquest of Belgium; but by the autumn the divisions between the allies and the dispersal of effort which the Dunkirk attack involved had led to defeat and disappointment all along the front. George III's second son the Duke of York, who commanded the British forces, had to admit to his father by September that he had given up all hope of capturing Dunkirk. 'The distress of mind I feel,' he wrote, 'is more than I can express.' Pitt showed more resilience, even though unkind critics were beginning to suggest that his high-handed interference in military matters had prejudiced the campaign. In July he was plunged in depression, fearing 'some melancholy event either on sea or land', but in September there came the cheering news that the great French naval base of Toulon, home of France's Mediterranean fleet, had surrendered to a British naval force in return for a promise of protection against the revolutionary government in Paris. Those who saw the war as a crusade wanted every available man to be hurried to Toulon: here at last was Britain's opportunity to carry out her mission and rid France of revolution. But Pitt, who saw the war as a struggle against the colonial power of France rather than as an exercise in political purification, was reluctant to divert forces from his chief concern that year, which was the seizure of French islands in the West Indies. Reinforcements were slow to arrive in Toulon, which was recaptured by revolutionary forces in December after a punishing artillery bombardment organised by a young French captain called Napoleon Bonaparte.

By this time there was fierce criticism of Pitt, especially among the French royalist exiles. They bitterly resented his refusal to recognise Louis XVI's eight-year-old son as the new King of France – a refusal which contrasted oddly with George III's declaration of October 1793 inviting the French to 'join

OVERLEAF The Light Horse and Dragoon Guards fighting the French at Landrecies, 1794.

the standard of an hereditary monarchy'. Although the royal declaration said that 'the internal situation of France obstructs the conclusion of a solid and permanent treaty', there were grounds for thinking that Pitt would come to terms with the revolutionary regime if only it would give up enough colonies. The campaigns of 1794 intensified these suspicions, for there was a sharp contrast between Britain's brilliant successes in the West Indies and her total failure to sustain the allied cause in Europe, where the French overran both Belgium and the Dutch Republic. Basically Pitt's strategy was that employed by his father more than thirty years before: while he used the bulk of Britain's own forces to make conquests from France in the colonial sphere, he subsidised allies in Europe to attack her along her own frontiers. Over £2 million was spent on subsidies in 1794, but there seemed to be very little to show for it. While the allies and exiles who received it complained of Britain's concentration on colonial conquests, the British taxpayers who provided it complained of allied duplicity and urged still greater concentration on theatres of war outside Europe. The one question which was hardly ever asked, let alone answered, was the really vital one: how was the balance of power in the Low Countries, the essential link between Europe and the colonial world, to be re-established if Britain and her European allies continued to distrust each other?

Dissension and distrust within the alliance were matched by dissension and distrust within Pitt's own cabinet. Henry Dundas put his finger on the real nature of the trouble in July 1794, when Pitt asked him to be war minister in the government reshuffle which had to be undertaken when the Portland Whigs came into the ministry. Having pointed out that 'the operations of war are canvassed and adjusted in cabinet', Dundas went on to say that even if there were to be somebody with the title of war minister 'not a person living would ever look upon him or any other person but yourself as the war minister'. In other words, Pitt's ascendancy was such that even in matters in which he could not get his own way it would be assumed that he had done so and he would have to bear the responsibility. In the end two Secretaries at War were appointed, Dundas himself and William Windham, one of the Portland Whigs. And Pitt's cousin Lord Grenville, who had succeeded Leeds as Foreign Secretary, also had to have a say in the conduct of the war in so far as it concerned our relations with our allies. It was not an easy team to manage.

And then of course there was the King. When the war began he supported Pitt's point of view, which was that peace could come either as a result of the overthrow of the French revolutionaries or if 'the issue of the present war shall be such as, by weakening their power of attack, shall strengthen our power of resistance'. But as things got worse George III, characteristically, grew more determined and more uncompromising. The disasters of 1794, and more particularly the faithlessness of the allies, made him increasingly anxious that Great Britain should declare herself to be fighting a holy war in defence of monarchy and established religion. He bitterly resented the use of British troops for colonial conquest rather than for the crushing of France herself – 'any considerable diminution of the forces under the command of my son on the Continent at present must greatly defeat the power of advancing into Austrian Flanders', he told Dundas – and he was deeply hurt when Pitt insisted at the end of the year that the only way to preserve the alliance was to take the command away from the Duke of York. George gave way, but he made it clear that he thought that his favourite son was being made a scapegoat for what he called 'the conduct of Austria, the faithlessness of Prussia and the cowardice of the Dutch'. And he insisted that his speech to Parliament should be drafted in 'a language of resolution to prosecute a war that every tie of religion, morality and society

A Gillray cartoon entitled 'Promised Horrors of the French Invasion' showing Fox scourging Pitt.

Pubd. July 6th 1795. by H. Humphrey No. 37. New Bond Street

The BRITISH-BUTCHER,

Supplying JOHN-BULL with a Substitute for BREAD. Vide, Message to Lord Mayor.

BILLY the BUTCHER's advice to JOHN BULL.

Since Bread is so dear, (and you say you must Eat,)
For to save the Expence, you must live upon Meat;
And as Twelve Pence the Quartern you can't pay for Bread
Get a Crown's worth of Meat, — it will serve in its stead.

not only authorises but demands'. There was to be no more talk of a negotiated peace with the French revolutionaries, however many colonies they might be prepared to yield. Whatever other princes might do, the King of England would do his duty.

In 1795 things went from bad to worse. The Prussians, the Dutch and the Spaniards all made their peace with France and even the Austrian alliance was only retained at the cost of an enormous loan of more than £4 million. The French royalist exiles proved almost as expensive: they insisted on mounting an invasion of Brittany which cost over £1 million and which was such a disastrous failure that opposition leaders accused Pitt of deliberately sending the French noblemen to their deaths. In June 1795 the ten-year-old Louis XVII died in prison in Paris and the Comte de Provence assumed the title of Louis XVIII. He took the opportunity to issue a manifesto saying that he intended to punish the revolutionaries mercilessly and re-establish the old order of things in France – a declaration which made him an even more embarrassing ally than before and reduced still further the chances of a negotiated peace. The appalling weather in June, which helped to hasten the death of the young Louis XVII, also produced a critical situation in England. All over the country crops were blasted by the intense cold and lambs died in the fields. By August bread prices had risen to famine levels. Monster demonstrations and meetings were held in London and other towns, at which many thousands of people gathered to demand radical reform and the dismissal of Pitt and his colleagues. Pitt himself by no means underestimated the seriousness of his position. He knew that the discontent ran very deep and he had no illusions about the extent to which his own policies were to blame for it. At the end of October, during the state opening of Parliament, George III's coach was attacked by great crowds roaring 'No war, no Pitt, no King!' 'My head would be off in six months were I to resign,' Pitt remarked calmly to his friends at supper some weeks later. The war which was supposed to end a revolution in France was beginning to look as though it might be the means of beginning one in England.

Pitt acted with a firmness that bordered on desperation. As long ago as May 1794 a parliamentary secret committee which he had set up had reported that the various societies ostensibly formed to promote reform by peaceful means were in fact taking steps to distribute weapons to their members. Pitt had reacted

OPPOSITE A cartoon of 1795 on the high price of food.

John Bull is ground down by Pitt, 1795.

by suspending the Habeas Corpus Act, the traditional English safeguard against arbitrary imprisonment. Even George III was taken aback by this step: 'though it is highly right and necessary', he wrote, 'yet being a strong measure it is open to cavil'. Pitt had then gone on to indict a group of leading reformers for high treason. One of them, a London shoemaker called Thomas Hardy, had had his house attacked by a drunken crowd and his wife had died in childbirth as a result. Hardy and the other English reformers had been acquitted, but similar trials in Scotland had resulted in savage sentences of transportation and even death. Pitt's legal training told him that the Scottish judges were straining the law to its limits, but nevertheless he upheld them because of his fear of 'an enormous torrent of insurrection, which would sweep away all the barriers of government, law and religion'. Now, after the outrages of October 1795, he went still further and pushed through Parliament measures censoring the press and prohibiting all meetings of more than fifty people unless they were licensed by the magistrates. Most sinister of all, there was a terrifying proliferation of government spies and *agents provocateurs*, until even the administration itself – or at any rate the Treasury Solicitor, to whose office evidence for possible prosecutions for sedition came – had difficulty in distinguishing between the genuine revolutionary conspiracies and the fictitious plans put forward by its own agents. Even Samuel Rogers, an inoffensive and eminently cautious man, found himself dragged before the Privy Council because a man had come up to him in the street and talked about the possibility of a French invasion. 'We lived then under a reign of terror,' he wrote many years later.

'Pitt's reign of terror' has been roundly condemned by historians, and rightly so. In spite of his fears and his harshly repressive measures, 1796 was in fact a fairly quiet year and the ordinary people of England showed little inclination to seek a cure for their miseries in revolution. The contrast between Pitt's own life and the life of most of the people he governed was indeed spectacular. At Downing Street there were still dinners after the old style, with a 'first service' of thirteen different dishes, a 'second service' even more bounteous and a large and varied selection of desserts. One menu in September 1796 included turtle, mutton, ox tongue, chicken, veal, sausages, rabbit, venison, artichokes, vols-au-vent, partridges, turkey, cauliflower, sweetbreads, French beans, macaroni, broiled salmon, peas, pigeon, salad, trout, hare, jelly, scallops and several different kinds of meat pie. On this occasion the guests had only fruit and nuts for their dessert, though at other times there was usually 'a large piece of almond pastry'. A few

The distribution of charity at Durham.

months later a farmer in the Wye Valley gave his shepherd a sheep that had been struck by lightning, commenting that it would be the first time the man and his family had tasted meat for several months. Those who were out of work – and there were many thousands of them, for the bad harvests of the past few years had been accompanied by severe economic depression – lived on the very brink of starvation, since the crisis had strained the existing system of poor relief to a point where it could no longer feed them properly. They would have fared a little better if they could have trapped wild animals and birds to eat, but the landlords made sure that the ferocious laws against poaching were strictly enforced in order that there should be plentiful supplies of game for tables such as that over which Pitt presided in Downing Street. If social injustices and inequalities might be expected to breed revolution, then Pitt had good reason for his policy of repression. But they did not. Whether they were cowed or whether they were content, most of George III's subjects lived lives of quiet desperation which gave the lie to Pitt's talk of 'an enormous torrent of insurrection'.

Yet there is a certain amount of injustice and even perversity in the charges made against Pitt. By definition, his strong measures were bound to seem unnecessary once they had been successful: it is easy to believe that what did not happen could never have happened. Secure in their hindsight and in their mistaken belief that they need give no thought to the 'if's of history, historians have pointed out that many of the factors that produced revolution in France – above all the peasant uprisings in the summer of 1789 – did not exist in England. But it must be remembered that Pitt and his contemporaries did not think of revolution in terms of mass movements. They thought in terms of what had happened in Paris in 1789 and had nearly happened in London in 1780, at the time of the Gordon riots. They believed that if unscrupulous opposition politicians set out to exploit urban rioting, the sort of rioting that could easily grow out of mass meetings such as took place in the autumn of 1795, the result might be a collapse of government at the centre which might be accepted by the rest of the country as tamely as France had accepted the Parisian revolutions of the period since 1789. They did not know that they were living through a period which would change men's view of revolution, making them think of it as something caused by deep-seated social and economic causes rather than by

OPPOSITE The Gordon riots in 1780. This, the most serious breakdown of law and order of the century, was very much in the minds of those who framed the repressive legislation of the 1790s.

NEWGATE fired *by the* RIOTERS, *in* 1780.

In October 1795, the King's coach was mobbed.

specific and perhaps even accidental events. Therefore they concentrated on the specific events, seeking to prevent those which threatened order and property, the things which it was the business of any eighteenth-century government to defend.

It should also be remembered that Pitt did not react to the crisis simply by producing repressive measures. The King's speech to Parliament on 29 October 1795, the day of the great riots in London, had expressed a readiness to negotiate with the revolutionary rulers of France. It was Pitt's readiness rather than George III's and it led to a serious clash between King and minister. In January 1796 George III drew up a memorandum giving his reasons for opposing any attempt at making peace. He conceded that Pitt's public assurances of readiness to negotiate were 'perhaps useful steps at home', but insisted that if they were carried into effect they would prejudice the chances of a successful royalist counter-revolution in France – still in the King's eyes the real object of the war. This paper was circulated to other ministers as well as to Pitt and it was clear that the King was prepared to appeal to Pitt's more belligerent colleagues if the chief minister himself were to prove too pacific. Pitt went ahead and began peace negotiations, only to have them unscrupulously exploited by the French government. When further peace proposals in the summer of 1796 also failed, George III's attitude to his minister hardened still further. Opposition to Pitt was growing, both in Parliament and in the country, and the King had no intention of being lumbered with a minister who could make neither war nor peace. In February 1797 Joseph Farington noted in his diary that 'the opposition people would rather the French should succeed than Pitt continue after such mismanagement'. He added that even Pitt's supporters were beginning to complain openly of 'want of energy in government'. Three months later the King received an outspoken memorandum from an influential group of politicians saying that 'the present administration, from the irritation and alarm which now prevail in the public mind, are not likely to extricate the country from the difficulty in which it is involved'. Other and even more violent attacks on Pitt followed; and soon it was rumoured – not entirely without foundation, as it now appears – that George III was thinking of replacing Pitt with Henry Addington, the doctor's son who had once played with him at Burton Pynsent and who was now, as Speaker of the House of Commons, the very epitome of respectable mediocrity.

In spite of the complaints of 'want of energy', there was certainly no want of industry and application on Pitt's part. 'Mr Pitt is seldom seen even by his intimate acquaintances except in public,' wrote Farington, 'the pressure of affairs occupies him entirely.' For a few brief weeks at the end of 1796 and the beginning of 1797 he had a life of his own and his courtship of Eleanor Eden reached a point where there was actually talk of marriage. Then the curtain came down; he told Eleanor that there were 'decisive and insurmountable' obstacles to the match and he plunged once more into his work. It was a season of missed opportunities and cataclysmic disasters. The Austrians signed a preliminary treaty of peace with the French in April, leaving Great Britain entirely alone. In the same month the Channel fleet at Spithead mutinied, followed in May by the North Sea fleet at the Nore. Government agents looked in vain for evidence of collusion between the mutineers and the radicals on land: the mutinies placed the country in appalling danger – both the Dutch and the Spaniards, two of the greatest naval powers in Europe, had declared war against the British – but they did not seem to be part of the supposed revolution. And yet, revolution or no revolution, there was no doubt that the hand of war lay heavier upon Great Britain than

TREASURY
"To the Nuptial-Bower he led her, Blushing like the Morn." || The NUPTIAL-

A cartoonist's view of Pitt's brief romance with Eleanor Eden.

it had done for more than a century. There was little enough left of Pitt's bright hopes of a safe Patriot war against France's colonies. A large French force, sent to raise Ireland against the English, had been prevented from landing by a storm in Bantry Bay, while an attempted French invasion of Wales in February 1797 had ended in fiasco; but even these dangers, abortive though they were, had been enough to produce a run on the banks which forced Pitt to suspend cash payments. By the autumn the worst was over: the naval mutinies had been put down and the prophecies of impending bankruptcy had been proved false. But Pitt's hopes of peace were once again dashed when yet another series of negotiations broke down in humiliating circumstances. Britain stood alone, her diplomatic isolation matched by the political isolation of her prime minister as he faced the doubts of his colleagues and the growing distrust of his King.

7

THE LIVING LEGEND

ON 27 MAY 1798, THE DAY BEFORE his thirty-ninth birthday, Pitt fought a duel. At three o'clock in the afternoon, before an interested crowd of spectators on Putney Heath, the prime minister of Great Britain exchanged pistol shots with George Tierney, one of the few opposition politicians who still bothered to attend the House of Commons. Fox, together with most of his friends, had given up coming to debates some months before: since Parliament seemed to be, in Fox's phrase, 'deaf and blind' to the disastrous consequences of Pitt's war and Pitt's policy of repression, there seemed to be little point in keeping up the wordy struggle. The Foxites were annoyed with Tierney: by continuing to do the job he had been elected to do he had spoiled the effect of their gesture. And the result seemed to justify their annoyance, however frivolous their own neglect of parliamentary duties might have seemed. Pitt had behaved quite outrageously in the Commons, accusing Tierney of wishing to 'obstruct the defence of the country' simply because he had dared to criticise the government for rushing a navy recruiting Bill through Parliament in one day. Tierney had demanded satisfaction and now he had it: after one exchange in which both men missed, a second case of pistols was produced and Pitt fired his in the air. 'The business terminated without anything unpleasant to either party,' Pitt told his mother the following day, 'and in a way which left me perfectly satisfied both with myself and my antagonist, who behaved with great propriety.' He had good reason for his satisfaction. Englishmen had always loved a lord and they were delighted to be reminded that this overworked bureaucrat of a prime minister was after all the son of a nobleman, with all the swashbuckling instincts of his class. The Foxites had been proved right, though not perhaps quite in the way they had expected. Continued opposition to the war had merely given Pitt an opportunity to put himself into the same posture of gallant defiance which he had already persuaded his country to adopt.

A few months before things had been very different: the war had still been very unpopular and Pitt himself had been appalled by its impact upon the country. He had been seriously ill for weeks on end, suffering from weakness and from constant headaches and turning to scholarship and theology for consolation. He had read Bishop Tomline's *Exposition of the First of the Thirty-nine Articles* instead of the official documents – Tomline had once been his tutor and was later to be his biographer – and had astonished that prelate with his exact and

PREVIOUS PAGE Detail from a broadsheet in praise of Pitt.

voluminous knowledge of the Scriptures. But now, six months later, the war had become an exciting challenge instead of a leech-like obscenity. George III sent a message to Parliament on 20 April 1798 saying that there was 'considerable and increasing activity in the ports of France, Flanders and Holland, with the avowed design of attempting the invasion of His Majesty's dominions'; and at the same time men of property learned with alarm that the government had uncovered a conspiracy throughout the British Isles, a desperate design conceived by men who called themselves United Britons, United Scotsmen, United Irishmen and even – worst horror of all – United Englishmen. There had been dozens of arrests which in England and Scotland had had the effect of preventing any outbreak that might have been planned, but in Ireland it was clear that there was worse to come. At long last, it seemed, the French were about to do what they had been threatening to do for the past five and a half years: they would swoop down upon the British Isles and bring 'brotherhood and assistance' to all those who were working to overturn the established order of things. And Pitt, the appointed defender of that order, responded as energetically to the general challenge as he had to the specific one flung down by Tierney. Within a few months the talk of muddle and inefficiency had given way to admiration. The legend of Pitt the national hero, the 'pilot who weathered the storm', was born.

The first phase of the newly invigorated struggle was anything but heroic. The arrests in Ireland had been accompanied by a campaign of deliberate and unrestrained cruelty on the part of the troops there; and when the commander-in-chief in Ireland, Sir Ralph Abercromby, ventured to issue a general order condemning the atrocities committed by the soldiers his action was condemned by Pitt as being 'almost an invitation to a foreign enemy'. Abercromby was forced to resign and the army in Ireland continued its reign of licensed terror, flogging and torturing and killing as it went. The avowed object of its bloody progress was to prevent a rebellion and, in particular, to stop the Catholic peasantry of southern Ireland from giving any support to the United Irishmen, a largely Protestant revolutionary movement which had its main centres of strength in the north of the country. Instead the conduct of the troops drove the whole country to desperation and ensured that when the uprising came it would draw support from all religious communities. Goaded by the outrages of the soldiers, the leaders of the United Irishmen decided not to wait for the long-promised aid from France. They made an abortive attempt to seize Dublin and then they issued instructions for a general insurrection. By the time Pitt fought his duel with Tierney it was clear that Ireland was in a state of rebellion. 'I trust that as the sword is drawn it will not be returned into the sheath until the whole country has submitted without condition,' wrote the King grimly, 'the making any compromise would be perfect destruction.' There was no compromise and no mercy. Both the authorities and the rebels slaughtered and tortured indiscriminately. The government forces invented a new form of torture known as 'pitch-capping': a mixture of pitch and gunpowder was daubed on the victim's head and then set alight. The rebels, who could not afford to waste gunpowder, contented themselves with impaling loyalists on pikes.

On his thirty-ninth birthday, at the same time as he wrote to his mother to tell her about his duel, Pitt sent a letter to his old friend John Pratt who now, as Lord Camden, was Lord Lieutenant of Ireland. It was the first time he had written since the news of a general uprising had come through, yet there was a curious lack of surprise in his letter, a matter-of-fact acceptance which almost suggested that he had known in advance what was going to happen. There was a lot about the duel, comparatively little about the insurrection. 'I trust you are mastering successfully a great crisis,' he wrote. 'Cannot crushing the rebellion be followed by an Act appointing commissioners to treat for an Union?' Evidence of this sort, coming on top of the months of deliberate ill-treatment and provocation by the troops, has led generations of Irishmen and some Englishmen to believe that Pitt himself planned the rebellion in cold blood in order to push through a union and destroy the last vestiges of Ireland's freedom. Certainly in Ireland, as in England, the multiplicity of government spies meant that the genuine plans of the insurgents and the fictitious schemes of the *agents provocateurs* ran into one another and became hopelessly confused. It is also true that the Lord Lieutenant and his ministers at Dublin Castle, who formed the government of Ireland, were anxious that if there was to be a revolt it should be a premature one, sparked off before rather than after the threatened arrival of French troops. But beyond that it is impossible to go. The gravest charge against Pitt is not that he had some diabolical deep-laid plan for Ireland, but that he had no consistent Irish policy at all. If his thoughts turned to a union it was because it was a course into which he had been driven, not a course he had marked out in advance.

Pitt's view of the Irish problem was based on the assumption that the real danger came from the Protestant radicals, men of some property and standing in their own country who nevertheless felt that they were unjustly excluded from the inner ring of placemen and other office-holders who surrounded the government at Dublin Castle. Like the English independent country gentlemen who were in his eyes the prototypes for all Patriot political behaviour, they were formidable precisely because they had social standing without their fair share – or without what they considered their fair share – of political influence. The Catholic peasantry, on the other hand, were essentially loyalist and could be won over from the Protestant troublemakers by timely concessions. This assumption seemed to be strengthened by the French revolution: Irish Catholics, and especially the Irish Catholic clergy, were horrified by the attacks on the Church in France and became increasingly suspicious of those Protestant radicals who coupled resistance to English rule with talk of revolution. In 1793 Pitt pushed through the Irish Parliament, in the face of considerable opposition from the office-holders at Dublin Castle, a measure to give the vote in the Irish counties to Catholic freeholders. Since they could only vote for Protestants – Catholics could no more sit in the Parliament at Dublin than in the Parliament at Westminster – it was a meaningless and foolish concession. Wolfe Tone, the Protestant founder of the United Irishmen, said that it simply meant that 'the wretched tribe of forty-shilling freeholders' were 'driven to market' by their landlords. It soon became clear that the measure had embittered the divisions it was intended to heal: the Catholics now clamoured for genuine emancipation, which would allow them to hold offices and sit in Parliament, while the Protestant governing class closed ranks against them. Only within the ranks of the United Irishmen, who were opposed to the English connection altogether, was there effective Protestant support for the Catholic demands.

The situation was made worse in 1795 when Pitt allowed Earl Fitzwilliam, a member of the newly recruited Portland Whigs, to go to Ireland as Lord Lieutenant and proclaim his support for complete Catholic emancipation. George III, who had originally supported the idea of sending Fitzwilliam, was appalled: after taking advice from the Archbishop of

OVERLEAF The Battle of Wexford, 5 June 1798.

Canterbury, the Lord Chief Justice and the Lord Chancellor, he decided that to grant Catholic emancipation would be to violate his coronation oath. He told Pitt that 'the subject is beyond the decision of any cabinet of ministers' – an ominous declaration, far more uncompromising than his pronouncements on the vexed question of peace with France. The future of Ireland was clearly going to be decided by the conscience of the King and not by the cogitations of his ministers. Pitt hastily recalled Fitzwilliam, but the damage had already been done. The British government had done too little to satisfy the Catholics but quite enough to alarm the Protestants. Above all, it had acted in a way which suggested either crass inconsistency or cunning duplicity. If it had merely divided its enemies the charge of duplicity might be convincing; but since it had also divided or alienated any friends it might have had in Ireland the alternative charge seems nearer the truth. The 1798 rebellion was the product of British ineptitude, not of British intrigue.

The crushing of the rebellion was indeed followed, as Pitt had hoped, by a move for a union. 'Mr Pitt has in my opinion saved Ireland,' wrote the King in June 1798, as the government forces closed in on the rebels' last strongholds in County Wexford, 'and the new Lord Lieutenant must not lose the present moment of terror for frightening the supporters of the Castle into an union with this country; and no further indulgences must be granted to the Roman Catholics'. The loyalists' moment of terror seemed to have passed when the rebel camp at Vinegar Hill was captured on 21 June; but two months later the long-awaited French force landed in County Mayo in the west of Ireland. Its commander, General Humbert, had been led to expect that the Irish peasantry would flock to join their liberators, but instead he found himself opposed by Catholic militiamen enlisted in the service of the government. The new Lord Lieutenant, Lord Cornwallis, was doing his best to restrain the worst excesses of the loyalist forces and also to conciliate the Catholics. While his generals forced Humbert to surrender, he himself worked tirelessly to persuade the Protestant ascendancy at Dublin Castle that the only answer to Ireland's problems was a union accompanied by complete Catholic emancipation. And yet by the end of the year, when the last stirrings of rebellion had finally been stamped out, even Cornwallis had come round to thinking that union must come first, to be followed by emancipation. 'The Catholics,' he wrote

The Battle of Vinegar Hill, 27 June 1798.

in January 1799, 'if offered equality without an union, will probably prefer it to equality with an union, for in the latter case they must ever be content with inferiority; in the former, they would probably by degrees gain ascendancy.' In that sentence was the whole core of the Irish problem and of the Irish tragedy. At Westminster, swamped by the overwhelming majority of Protestant members from England and Scotland, the Irish Catholics could do no harm; but if they were allowed to sit in a separate Irish Parliament in Dublin their numerical superiority would enable them to take over the country. Once given emancipation, they would have no further motive to support union. It was this consideration that led almost every eighteenth-century Englishman involved in Ireland to move sooner or later from plain speaking to something dangerously like trickery. Union – or, for that matter, any other conceivable solution to the Irish problem – could only be achieved by holding out false hopes and false fears.

Pitt remained convinced that the trickery was the work of other men. When the Irish Parliament turned down his proposals for union in January 1799 he told Cornwallis that this was 'the effect of prejudice and cabal'. A few days later he made an impressive speech in the Commons at Westminster, declaring that 'No man can say that in the present state of things, and while Ireland remains a separate kingdom, full concessions could be made to the Catholics without endangering the state and shaking the constitution of Ireland to its centre'. It was not exactly a promise, but it was certainly a shrewd piece of tactics: the Catholics could take it to mean that *if* they agreed to union they might achieve emancipation, while the Protestants might well think that *unless* they agreed to union the British government might be forced into concessions which could shake the constitution. In Ireland Viscount Castlereagh, chief secretary to the Dublin Castle administration, won the borough-mongers and office-holders over to the idea of union by assuring them that they would get proper compensation for the political influence and lucrative places which they would lose when Ireland ceased to have her own Parliament. His promises have been described as bribery, though to an age which regarded office and influence as forms of property there was nothing illicit about them – indeed, some of those who were most heavily compensated were those who had opposed the union. But as a result of Castlereagh's work they were in a minority when the proposals for union were brought up again. The Act of Union was approved by both Parliaments in the spring and summer of 1800 and the United Kingdom of Great Britain and Ireland came into being on 1 January 1801. It only remained to see how far Pitt considered himself committed to Catholic emancipation and what – if anything – he would do about it.

By this time there were other things to think about as well as Ireland. 'I fear it is clear,' wrote a young English lawyer travelling on the continent, 'that the Sun of England's glory is set.' He was writing on the day after the new United Kingdom came into existence, but it was not the new bond with the Irish that was the cause of his depression. The war was going badly again: if anything things were even worse than they had been in the dreadful summer and autumn of 1797. The threatened invasion of 1798, the challenge that had revived Pitt's popularity as surely as it had revived the spirits of most of his countrymen, had not materialised. Instead the French government had sent General Bonaparte, its most successful and most popular and potentially most dangerous servant, to cut Britain's links with India by invading Egypt. On his way he had captured Malta, a Mediterranean island which the

Russians had always regarded as being under their special protection. When Bonaparte had actually landed in Egypt and had begun to win startling victories there, posing as the new saviour of Islam, the Russians had become seriously alarmed and had been relieved to hear that the British Admiral Nelson had destroyed Bonaparte's fleet at the Battle of the Nile in August 1798. Pitt had been enabled to create a new coalition of European powers, including the Emperors of Austria and Russia as well as the King of Naples and the Sultan of Turkey. There had been more huge subsidies for the Austrians and the German princes, more fierce criticisms from the British taxpayer. In 1799 Pitt had even managed to get the British Parliament to accept an income tax; but it was not long before his critics were able to revive the old charges of mismanagement and misappropriation and misuse of the vast new revenues which he had raised. In 1799 there had been victories: the Austrians and the Russians between them had driven the French out of Italy and even the British themselves had had some limited successes in the Dutch Republic. But by 1800 the coalition was on the point of collapse, thanks to the staggering achievements of General Bonaparte, who had in November 1799 overthrown the government of France and established himself as a virtual dictator. When Pitt came to review his political position in the summer and autumn of 1800 it was the new constitution of France, rather than the new constitution of the United Kingdom, that dominated his thinking.

His initial reactions to Bonaparte's rise to power were hesitant and uncertain. He told George III on 25 November 1799 that negotiations for peace should now be reopened, but the King was hard to convince: he had already told the Foreign Secretary that 'the recent revolution at Paris shows how very unstable the republic was, and the present violent change cannot possibly hold long, but every revolution there is advantageous to the opinions of those who wish the restoration of royalty'. When Bonaparte sent a personal letter to George III suggesting that their two countries should now come to terms, Pitt was quick to point out to Dundas that it was 'very civil in its terms, and seems, by the phrase which describes the two countries as being both more powerful than their security requires, to point at their being willing to give up at least a part of the French conquests if we do the same as to ours'. Yet by the end of the year he had decided that peace negotiations should, after all, be put off for the time being; and the debates in Parliament at the beginning of 1800 seemed to suggest that Great Britain was waiting to see whether Bonaparte could establish really strong government before she decided whether or not she would negotiate with him. If so, then she was to find that he met her requirements more quickly and more successfully than she had expected: his brilliant victory at Marengo in northern Italy in June 1800 not only established his complete control of France beyond any doubt but also spelt the end of Pitt's coalition. By the end of July, when the parliamentary session was brought to a close, it looked as though Britain's last chance for an honourable negotiated peace had come.

Pitt was ill during the parliamentary recess, iller than he had ever been in his life before. He was in almost constant pain and his habit of regular sleep, his greatest strength in times of stress, seemed to have deserted him. His cabinet was bitterly divided over the question of peace or war, quite apart from the even more ferocious divisions which were likely to appear if he once

Napoleon's campaign in Egypt:
ABOVE Napoleon at the Battle of Aboukir, July 1799.
LEFT The Battle of the Pyramids, July 1798.

broached the delicate subject of Catholic emancipation. Nor did his troubles end there. 'After all,' he told Addington, 'the question of peace or war is not in itself half so formidable as that of the scarcity with which it is necessarily combined, and for the evils and growing dangers of which I see no adequate remedy.' His doctor told him that he had no hope of surviving the coming session of Parliament unless he had a proper holiday, preferably at Cheltenham or Bath or some other watering-place. In the end he decided to spend a few weeks with Addington at his house near Reading. He was near to breaking-point, mentally as well as physically, and his host regarded him as a patient rather than a guest. 'He wants rest and *consolation*,' said Addington to his younger brother, the same Hiley who had once flogged Pitt at Chatham's command, 'and I trust he will find both here.' Both brothers prepared to take the prime minister under their wing, soothing his anxieties and tactfully limiting his supplies of port wine.

Pitt's political future, as well as the future of the war in Europe and the troubles of Ireland, may well have been decided during those deceptively uneventful weeks of convalescence at Addington's home. He had time to think and he also had time to take stock of his host. He had secured Addington's election as Speaker of the House of Commons in 1789, at which time the defeated opposition candidate for the post had remarked sourly that the new Speaker was 'the son of Lord Chatham's physician and is in fact a sort of dependent to the family. The Chair has hitherto been filled by persons of quite a different description.' And yet George III, who was a stickler for social precedence and had always been used to being served by men of noble birth, had taken a liking to Addington. In 1797 he had even thought of making him prime minister in Pitt's stead; and later on, after Pitt's resignation, there were those who said that Addington had been 'undermining Pitt with the King' for at least two years before he finally replaced him. Gossips less friendly to Pitt insisted on the other hand that the latter had deliberately used Addington as a cat's-paw, resigning his place to him when things got difficult and expecting to have it back for the asking when the skies cleared again. Probably neither accusation was entirely just, but both had an element of truth in them. Both men were politicians, ambitious and convinced of their own abilities, and both were conscious of the hazards and uncertainties of serving George III. They were also conscious of the even greater uncertainties of a possible new

George III reviewing the volunteers in June 1799, by S.W. Reynolds after R.K. Porter.

reign. They both saw a lot of the sixty-two-year-old King and they were aware that his health might give way at any moment, leaving the political world exposed to the unpredictable vagaries of the Prince of Wales.

Pitt's father had been in a strikingly similar position forty years before, just before the death of George II and the accession of George III. He too had been the Patriot minister of an old and obstinate King, waging a war which was enervating and difficult to bring to an end. In his case peace had been hard to obtain not because of defeat but because of victory – he had confessed grimly to his intimates that his problem was to find

OVERLEAF Volunteers lined up in Hyde Park for the King's review.

which of his conquests he could give up without being hanged for it – but the net result had been very much the same. Peace had had to be made and it had blighted the careers of those who had made it. Pitt the elder had got out in time to avoid the odium of making peace, but he had not got out in time to avoid offending the new King when he came to the throne. If his son was to learn from his example he must copy the success and avoid the failure. If he was to go at all he must go now.

There was little to cheer him when he returned to Downing Street. Parliament had to be summoned earlier than usual because of the food shortage and the widespread distress throughout the country; and it met in an ugly mood, ready to blame the administration for failures abroad and discontent at home. The Russians, once again on the French side now that the British had recaptured Malta, organised an 'armed neutrality' of powers in the Baltic which threatened to bring British trade there to a standstill. Austria, disastrously defeated by the French within a few miles of her own capital city, made peace early in 1801. And then, on 28 January 1801, the moment of crisis arrived. Either by chance or design, either through the malice of Pitt's enemies or the carelessness of his friends, George III received garbled and exaggerated accounts of the ministry's intention to grant Catholic emancipation. 'What is it that this young lord has brought over which they are going to throw at my head?' stormed the King, referring to Castlereagh's recent arrival from Ireland. 'The most Jacobinical thing I ever heard of! I shall reckon any man my personal enemy who proposes any such measure.' The outburst was premature: the cabinet was far too bitterly divided to throw Catholic emancipation at the King's head, while even Pitt himself was not yet fully committed to it publicly. But the challenge had now been thrown down and it was perhaps with relief that the exhausted prime minister took it up. Like his father before him, Pitt found it difficult to believe that ordinary human beings could so snarl up their affairs that they could not accept the obvious rectitude of the courses recommended to them. It seemed to him intolerable that the path which he deemed to be right should have led him into a position in which he must either trick the Irish or trick his King. He had no wish to do either and so he prepared to resign.

Resignation proved to be anything but simple. He expressed his regretful determination to the King on 3 February and George accepted it, equally regretfully, two days later; but before the new ministry could be put together the King fell ill again. He had been consulting with Addington even before he received Pitt's letter of resignation and there was no doubt that Addington was to be Pitt's successor. But there was a certain incredulity in political circles, an inability to accept that the son of the great Chatham was really giving way to the son of a provincial physician, and this hampered the task of constructing a new administration. Politicians watched as if mesmerised, unable to believe that this charade was intended to be taken seriously. Pitt agreed to stay on until the new arrangements were complete and he even introduced his budget on 18 February, five days after the King was first taken ill. That same evening George wrote him a short but affectionate letter, addressing him for the first and only time as 'My dear Pitt'. When the King's illness became critical at the end of the month there were the inevitable whisperings to the effect that the whole crisis was a put-up job designed to cut Pitt's losses in the event of the King's death. Nevertheless, the Prince of Wales agreed to regard Pitt as the effective prime minister and there were preparations to put through Parliament a Regency Bill on the lines of that drafted by Pitt in 1788-9. But the King recovered and at last, on 14 March, William Pitt delivered up the seals of office which he had held for more than seventeen years. Some days before he had been distressed to hear that the King had accused him of precipitating the royal illness by bringing up the question of Catholic emancipation. He had therefore sent to the King, before his actual resignation, a solemn assurance that he would never again raise the question as long as the King lived.

By promising never to raise the Catholic question Pitt raised another and even more teasing one, a question which puzzled men at the time and has puzzled them ever since. If emancipation was to be dropped, why resign at all? He might feel that he owed it to the Irish Catholics to do so, but he would do their cause little good by binding himself not to help them in the future. To resign because your advice has not been accepted may be honourable, but to resign even when you agree that it shall never be accepted in the future seems rather less so. Most practical politicians thought at the time that the resignation was not a matter of principles at all but of personalities; if Pitt and Addington could have come to terms, if the one had been less haughty and the other less flushed by his sudden rise to eminence, a joint administration in which both of them

PROCLAMATION OF PEACE AT THE ROYAL EXCHANGE, LONDON, APRIL 29, 1802.

BY THE KING. A PROCLAMATION.

GEORGE R.

WHEREAS a Definitive Treaty of Peace and Friendship between Us, the French Republick, His Catholick Majesty, and the Batavian Republick, hath been concluded at Amiens, on the Twenty-seventh Day of March last, and the Ratifications thereof have been duly exchanged: In Conformity thereunto, We have thought fit hereby to command that the same be published throughout all Our Dominions: And We do declare to all Our loving Subjects Our Will and Pleasure, that the said Treaty of Peace and Friendship be observed inviolably as well by Sea as Land, and in all Places whatsoever; strictly charging and commanding all Our loving Subjects to take Notice hereof, and to conform themselves thereunto accordingly.

Given at Our Court at Windsor, the 26th Day of April, 1802, in the 42d Year of Our Reign.

GOD SAVE THE KING.

CEREMONY.

ST. JAMES'S, APRIL 29, 1802.

THE Officers of Arms, Serjeants at Arms, with their Maces and Collars; the Serjeant-Trumpeter, with his Mace and Collar; the Trumpets, Drum-Major, and Drums, and the Knight Marshal, and Knight Marshal's Men, assembled this Day, at Half past Ten o'Clock in the Forenoon, in the Stable Yard, St. James's; and the Officers of Arms, being habited in their respective Tabards, and mounted, a Procession was made, at Twelve o'Clock, from thence to the Palace-Gate, where George Harrison, Esq. Norroy King of Arms, read His Majesty's Proclamation of Peace; which being done, a Procession was made to Charing-Cross, in the following Order, viz.

A Party of Life Guards, to clear the Way.
Beadles of Westminster, Two and Two, with Staves.
Constables of Westminster, in like Manner.
High Constable, on Horseback, with his Staff.
Officers of the High Bailiff of Westminster, on Horseback, with White Wands.
High Bailiff and Deputy Steward, on Horseback.
Three Knight Marshal's Men, Bearers of the Verge, with Maces.
Eight Knight Marshal's Men, Two and Two.
Sir James Bland Burges, Bart. Knight Marshal, on Horseback, with his Baton.
Drums.
Drum Major.
Trumpets.
Serjeant Trumpeter, in his Collar, with his Mace.
Francis Martin, Gent.
Blue Mantle Pursuivant.

	James Cathrow, Gent. Rouge Dragon Pursuivant.	Joseph Hawker, Gent. Rouge Croix Pursuivant.	
Serjeant at Arms.	George Naylor, Esq. York Herald.	John Atkinson, Esq. Somerset Herald.	Serjeant at Arms.
Serjeant at Arms.	Edmund Lodge, Esq. Lancaster Herald.	George Martin Leake, Esq. Chester Herald.	Serjeant at Arms.
Serjeant at Arms.	Francis Townsend, Esq. Windsor Herald.	Ralph Bigland, Esq. Richmond Herald.	Serjeant at Arms.

Norroy King of Arms, between two Serjeants at Arms.
A Party of Life Guards.

Life Guards, who flanked the Procession. — Life Guards, who flanked the Procession.

At Charing-Cross Richmond Herald read the Proclamation aloud; and the Procession moved on, in the same Order to Temple-Bar; the Gates of which being shut, Blue Mantle Pursuivant of Arms left the Procession, and, accompanied by Two Trumpets, preceded by Two Life Guards to clear the Way, rode up to the Gates, and, after the Trumpets had sounded thrice, he knocked with his Cane. Being asked by the City Marshal from within, "*Who comes there?*" he replied, "*The Officers of Arms, who demand Entrance into the City to publish his Majesty's Proclamation of Peace.*" The Gates being opened, he was admitted alone, and the Gates were immediately shut again. The City Marshal, preceded by his Officers, conducted him to the Lord Mayor, (who was on Horseback, and, with the Aldermen, Recorder, and Sheriffs, attended within the Gate,) to whom he shewed His Majesty's Warrant, which his Lordship having read, returned; and gave Directions to the City Marshal to open the Gates, who, attending the Pursuivant back, opened them accordingly, and, on leaving him, said, "*Sir, the Gates are open.*" The Trumpets and Life Guards being in waiting, conducted him to his Place in the Procession, which then moved on into the City, except the Officers of Westminster, who filed off and retired as they came to Temple-Bar.

At the End of Chancery-Lane Windsor Herald read the Proclamation. Then the Lord Mayor, with the City Officers, joined the Procession, immediately after the Officers of Arms, in the following Order, viz.

Four Constables,
Six Marshal's Men, Three and Three, on Foot.
Six Trumpets, Three and Three.
Band of Music,
The Two City Marshals, on Horseback.

Sheriffs' Officers on Foot.	The Two Sheriffs, on Horseback.	Sheriffs' Officers on Foot.

Sword and Mace-Bearers, on Horseback.

Porter, in a Black Gown, with his Staff.	The LORD MAYOR, on Horseback, bearing his Sceptre of Office.	Ward Beadle with the Ward Mace.

Lord Mayor's Household, on Foot.
Six Footmen, Three and Three.
His Lordship's State Coach, drawn by Six White Horses.
The Aldermen (according to Seniority) and the Recorder, in their Coaches.
Carriages of the Sheriffs.
Officers of the City, in Carriages, according to Seniority.
The Volunteer Corps of the City.
Life Guards.

Life Guards, in Single File. — Life Guards, in single File.

At the End of Wood-Street, where the Cross formerly stood, in Cheapside, the Proclamation was read by Chester Herald. The Procession moving on to the Royal Exchange, the Proclamation was there read, for the last Time, by Lancaster Herald.

The Lord Mayor having, upon this joyful Occasion, convened the several Volunteer Corps of the City in order to add to the Splendour of the Ceremony, as well as to deliver to them the Thanks of His Majesty and the Honourable House of Commons for their Services during the War, it became necessary to extend the Procession to Aldgate; whence it returned, through Fenchurch-Street, and up Gracechurch-Street, and passed again through Cornhill, to the Mansion-House; from whence the Procession of the Officers of Arms, Knight Marshal, Drums and Trumpets, and Life Guards, returned through St. Paul's Church-Yard.

The Acclamations of Joy were general from many Thousands of Spectators, who filled all the Streets through which the Procession passed; and, in the Evening, the universal Satisfaction of the People was manifested by the Display of splendid Illuminations in all Parts of the Metropolis.

The proclamation of peace following the Treaty of Amiens, 1802.

served could easily have been arranged. But in either case, principles or personalities, one thing was certain: Pitt's eyes were on the future. He had extricated himself from an impossible situation and he had given himself a breathing-space in which he might be able to regain his old vigour of mind and body. And the only price he had paid had been a promise not to do the thing which in any case he would never be able to do – force George III into accepting Catholic emancipation. He had not, however, made any promises about what he would or would not do in the next reign; and since he was twenty-one years younger than the King he might be forgiven for thinking that the transition from one reign to the next, the problem which had almost destroyed his father's political career, would be an important one for him also. He was not to know that George III would outlive him by fourteen years.

A few days after Pitt's resignation Addington suggested rather hesitantly to the King's doctor that he should try to get the royal consent for the reopening of peace negotiations. To his great surprise the King was reported to be quite eager for peace and said that he had long wished for it. A little later the Prince of Wales was astonished to hear his father say that he would soon abdicate the throne and retire to Hanover to die. This plan was soon abandoned; but if the King ever entertained it seriously it might help to explain his sudden readiness to come to terms with the power which now dominated the whole of Europe. As a Genevese exile had reluctantly admitted to Farington some months before, there were now only two nations left in Europe: the British and the French. Addington duly made his peace with Bonaparte by the Treaty of Amiens in March 1802; and when Farington took the opportunity to go to Paris himself he found that public opinion there had narrowed Europe's problems down even further than his Genevese friend had done. It was not even a question of two nations but of two men: 'the French,' wrote Farington in his diary, 'have a high idea of Pitt and say he is the only man who can act against the ability of Bonaparte.' The House of Commons seemed to think the same. When some opposition members took the opportunity afforded by the peace to criticise the war in general, and Pitt in particular, there was a fierce reaction which led in the end to an alternative motion being carried, by an overwhelming majority, which expressed the gratitude of the House to Pitt for his 'great and important services to his country'. Still more impressive was the dinner

OVERLEAF
Walmer Castle, Pitt's official residence as Warden of the Cinque Ports.

organised by Pitt's friends in celebration of his forty-third birthday on 28 May 1802. Pitt himself declined to attend, but more than eight hundred guests drank to his health and sang *The Pilot that weathered the Storm*, a hymn of praise composed for the occasion by George Canning, one of Pitt's fiercest and ablest supporters. As well as proffering to Pitt 'the thanks of a people thy firmness has saved', the song looked forward almost with eagerness to a renewed outbreak of war with would sweep the hero back to power:

> And O! if again the rude whirlwind should rise
> The dawning of peace should fresh darkness deform,
> The regrets of the good and the fears of the wise
> Shall turn to the pilot that weathered the storm.

Certainly the pilot was well placed to watch for the storm-clouds. Back in 1792 the King had made him Warden of the Cinque Ports, an office he still held; and there was something splendidly symbolic about the way his official residence at Walmer Castle gazed out over the Kentish cliffs at the continent which the French now dominated so completely. Napoleon Bonaparte was already First Consul of France for life and soon he was to become Emperor of the French, setting up his brothers and the marshals of his army as subject kings in the other countries of Europe. He epitomised not merely the universalist aspirations of the French revolution but also the older and equally sweeping ambitions of the French monarchy. While the popular press in Britain affected to treat him as though he were a pygmy, a scowling little soldier who had risen to fame through the accidents of war, more intelligent and perceptive men realised that he was perhaps the greatest ruler Europe had ever seen – certainly the greatest in their lifetime. As well as understanding the problems that were involved in uniting Europe he also understood the threat that Great Britain posed to the unity of the continent. Throughout the eighteenth century there had been growing resentment in Europe of Britain's high-handed commercialism, her calm assumption that the pattern of things on the continent must be made to fit into the requirements of her trade rather than the other way about. Pitt's own father had done more than any other man to provoke and justify this resentment, which had united Europe against Britain during the War of American Independence and was now helping to unite her again under Napoleon. Pitt the son had been less imperious than Pitt the

OPPOSITE William Pitt by J. Hoppner.

father: he had always insisted that his war was simply for security. But since that security involved an insistence on keeping Europe disunited, on dividing the forces on the other side of the Channel so that Britain could continue to trade with impunity, there was still an irreconcilable confrontation which could lead only to war.

In fact the Warden of the Cinque Ports was feeling anything but warlike during the summer and autumn of 1802. He went riding and sailing and partridge-shooting and he acquired a farm for himself near Walmer, where he indulged the passion for 'improvements' and landscape gardening which he had inherited from his father. He felt his health and strength returning and he revelled in his new-found leisure, but he realised nevertheless that this idyllic life could not last. 'My new farm will keep me constantly employed for the remainder of the year,' he told Addington in September, 'or till *the pacificator of Europe* takes it into his head to send an army from the opposite coast to revenge himself for some newspaper paragraph.' Pitt knew well enough that Bonaparte's anger at attacks on him in the British press was not the fundamental reason for the steadily worsening relations between the two countries. The Treaty of Amiens was unworkable, a mere truce in recognition of a stalemate, because neither side would abandon its real or imagined right to interfere with the other. France could only control the land and yet she insisted on telling Britain what she could and could not do at sea – what colonies and naval bases she must give up, what ports she must trade with. Britain, whose strength was essentially naval and not military, reserved a right to settle the balance of power on land and to tell France what countries she could or could not march into. In these circumstances it was difficult to see how a renewal of war could be avoided, even if every British newspaper in print were forbidden to make fun of the First Consul of France.

By the time Parliament met again in November 1802 Pitt's friends were for the most part convinced that war was inevitable and that only he could conduct it. Canning rebuked the House of Commons for making light of Bonaparte and declared that it was precisely because of his greatness, 'the amazing ascendancy of his genius', that Great Britain needed a Pitt to match him. But Pitt was ill again: the improvement in his health brought about by the rural pursuits of Kent had proved short-lived and by mid-September his doctor had pronounced his condition to be critical. There was a recovery towards the

A crescent in Bath, where Pitt went to take the waters.

end of September, but it was decided nevertheless that Pitt must go to Bath to take the waters. He was very weak and his bloated face and shaking hands, signs of his heavy drinking, were becoming increasingly noticeable. 'It is said that since he quitted office he has indulged rather more freely in the use of wine,' wrote Farington. Politicians travelled back and forth between London and Bath trying to arrange some broadening of the administration, but Pitt showed little enthusiasm for their schemes. Quite apart from his physical condition there was still the time factor: it would be four or five years, he told his friends, before British finances were sufficiently recovered to bear the strain of a new war. Then, perhaps, it would be time for him to return. In the meantime he would keep his promise, made to the King and to Addington at the time of his resignation, not to oppose the existing administration. Yet the international situation grew steadily worse and by the spring of 1803 it was clear that there would be war. In April Pitt at last took action,

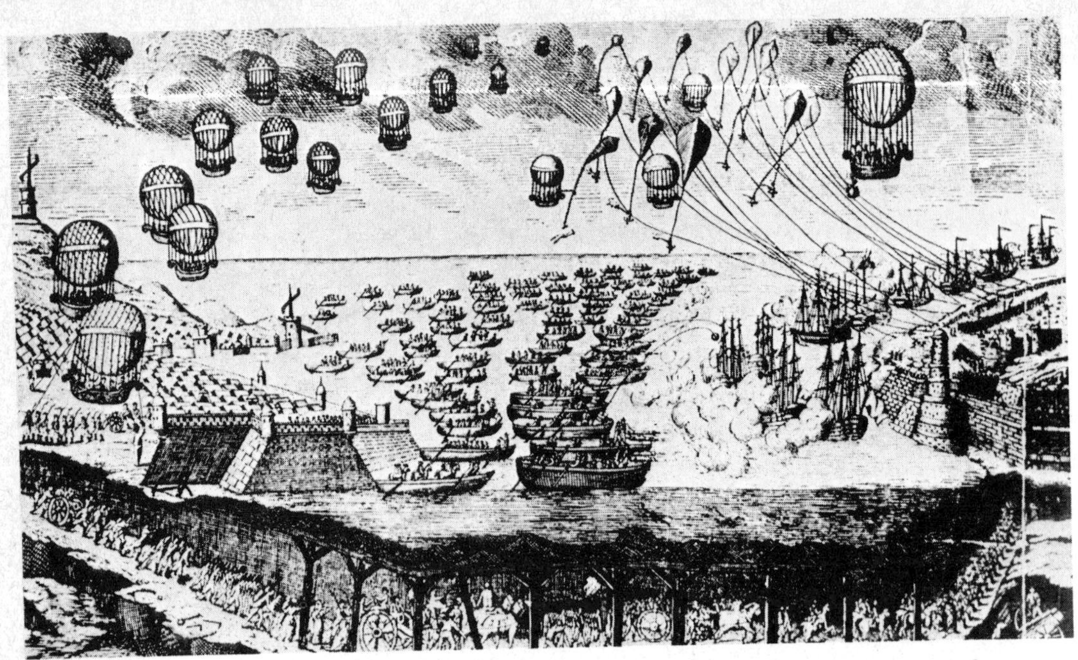

A French plan for the invasion of Britain by tunnel, sea and air.

canvassing the idea of a broadly-based ministry which should include Fox on the one hand and himself on the other. The negotiations proved disastrous: the Foxites felt themselves betrayed, Addington stood very much on his dignity and the King was furious at the presumption of this ex-prime minister who seemed to think he could dictate terms to his sovereign. Everyone blamed Pitt; and they continued to blame him for the rest of the parliamentary session, as he did his best to preserve his position after war had actually broken out again in May 1803. If he seemed eager to return to power he would offend his King; if he seemed reluctant he would disappoint his own followers. And so he made judicious speeches 'evading censure and refusing approbation' of the Addington ministry. For his pains he was dubbed a trimmer and a turncoat and accused of 'conduct below the dignity of his character'.

Throughout the summer, while Bonaparte prepared for the invasion of England, the Warden of the Cinque Ports busied himself with the defence of Kent. Even professional soldiers were impressed with his ability. 'He had paid such attention to military science,' they said, 'and his mind acted so powerfully upon it, that if he proceeded he would be the best general in the country.' But the French did not come. Bonaparte had told his navy minister within days of the outbreak of the war that 'we must have a model of a flat-bottomed boat able to transport a

Two inventions designed to carry Napoleon's troops over the Channel:
LEFT A balloon designed by Thilorière.
BELOW A floating fortress.

hundred men across the Channel. There would be a mortar in the bows and stern. . . .'; but when the projected invasion barges were actually built they proved almost totally useless. 'It is impossible to suppose for an instant that anything effective can be produced by such miserable tools,' wrote an English admiral, '. . . floored as this wretched vessel is, she cannot hug the wind but must drift bodily to leeward . . .' On land, however, the hastily assembled volunteer soldiers continued to drill. Even in December, when most people agreed that the real danger was past, Pitt could still write that he would be 'so constantly occupied all next week in going round to my different battalions that it will be impossible for me to think of going to town till the week after'. Nevertheless he did go to town within a few days and he took a vigorous part in the debates of the new session. Both his reputation and his strength seemed to have recovered remarkably since the spring. His cousin Grenville had now gone over to Fox, declaring that it was essential to work for a broadly based administration which would include all men of ability; but Pitt would not commit himself to a course of action which looked dangerously like forcing the King's hand. Instead he watched and waited, 'hanging aloof,' as one commentator put it, 'to pounce upon them all in due time'.

In the event it was the King who forced the hand of the politicians and not the other way about. He fell ill in February 1804 and it took him a long time to recover his strength, even though this time there was no question of his mind being affected. In these circumstances Pitt could not afford to hesitate any longer: if he continued to hold out against the idea of a coalition there might well be a coalition against him. The Prince of Wales was already planning an administration and even Addington's men, committed though they were to George III, had more in common with the Foxites than they had with Pitt. If death removed the King – and thus the King's veto on Fox – Pitt might find himself isolated. If on the other hand the King lived he would be better served by a definite move on Pitt's part than by the steady slide into political chaos which the present uncertainties were producing. In April Pitt and his followers voted against the ministry, along with Grenville and the Foxites, and later that month negotiations for the entry of Pitt into the administration were begun. The King remained loyal to Addington and was prepared to dissolve Parliament and fight a General Election in order to increase his majority; but Addington preferred to resign. Pitt made some token efforts to get George III to agree to a coalition including the Foxites, but he must have known that these attempts were doomed to failure: he had already hinted, in his letter to the King at the beginning of the negotiations, that if necessary he would be prepared to come in without Fox, and now George took advantage of that hint. There were bitter recriminations on all sides, but by this time it was generally agreed that Pitt was the only man who could hold British political life together for the time being, until the death of the King removed existing difficulties and made the long-awaited coalition ministry possible. On 18 May 1804, with the arrangements for the second Pitt administration almost complete, George III bade a kindly farewell to Addington. On the same day Napoleon Bonaparte proclaimed himself Emperor of the French.

The remaining months of Pitt's life belong to legend rather than to history. The facts are simple enough, stark and saddening: he struggled heroically, both against his own ill-health and against Napoleon's domination of the continent, and he failed. His European allies accepted his subsidies and then mis-spent them, making their peace with the triumphant Napoleon after their shattering defeat at Austerlitz in December 1805. The British navy won a magnificent victory under Lord Nelson off Cape Trafalgar in October of that year, but even this served only to restore rather than to break the stalemate: Napoleon could not move against Britain at sea any more, but Pitt could still not move against France on land. Efforts to re-establish the British bridgehead in the Dutch Republic came to nothing and the opportunities in Spain and Portugal, which were eventually to provide the British army with an effective entry into Napoleon's Europe, still lay in the future. All Pitt's administrative skill could make little impression on the cumbersome inadequacies of the War Office, while his record of success and efficiency in naval matters was marred by fierce opposition attacks on his friend Dundas, who was accused of dishonesty and corruption during his time as Treasurer of the Navy. When the House of Commons voted in April 1805 to impeach Dundas Pitt broke down and sat on the government front bench with tears running down his cheeks, his friends crowding round him to hide him from the contemptuous gaze of the triumphant opposition.

The struggle against Napoleon, frustrating and inconclusive though it was, did at least buy time: if Great Britain could not impose her will upon Europe she could at any rate preserve her

OVERLEAF Turner's painting of the Battle of Trafalgar.

Pitt and Napoleon carving up the world, 1805.

own independence and wait for the tide to turn. The struggle against ill-health had no such consolations. It was a losing battle and Pitt knew it. He became in those last few months intensely detached and aloof, as men often are when they have seen their own death clearly and unmistakably. Some of his colleagues were horrified by his changed character, which was said to be 'such that very few could associate with him, so repulsive is his manner'. Others were overawed: John Opie the

painter noted the 'extraordinary power of expression' in Pitt's face and another painter, Thomas Lawrence, was amazed to see the deference with which the prime minister was treated. At dinner at Lord Abercorn's he noticed 'how high above the rest Mr Pitt appeared to be in the consideration of the whole party. It did not prevent social conversation, but all seemed to be impressed with an awe of him. At times it appeared like boys with their master. When he spoke it was not extended to much talk, but rather pithy remarks and frequently sarcastic observations.' In some company he could still unbend, especially in that of children. At Bath in the autumn of 1805, when he had only a few weeks left to live and spent most of his time lying listlessly on a couch, he could still summon up the energy to play with the children of his friends. A little earlier, in 1804, he took part in a hilarious game with three small boys and with his niece Hester Stanhope, who kept house for him at that time. The others had to try to blacken his face with burnt cork while he fought them off with a cushion. When it was at its height Lord Castlereagh and Lord Liverpool were announced: they had come to see the prime minister on important business. One of the small boys later told how Pitt washed his face, interviewed his colleagues with icy disdain and then returned with obvious relish to the cushion and cork game. But such moments were rare: as Hester Stanhope herself later wrote, those last months of Pitt's life were made up almost entirely of overwork, irregular meals and heavy drinking. 'It was enough to kill a man,' she concluded, 'it was murder!'

It was indeed. Pitt drove himself relentlessly, his constant and ubiquitous attention to the business of government feeding upon itself. Yet in a sense all his unremitting labours were almost irrelevant: he had already transcended his own political career and had become more important as a symbol than as a statesman. The fact that the bearer of England's proudest name was wearing himself out in the war against Napoleon was enough to ennoble that war, turning a struggle for commercial pre-eminence into a crusade for all that Englishmen held dear. Pitt enabled his countrymen to transcend even their own insularity and to convince themselves that they were at one not only with the Irish and the Scots and the Welsh but also with the European races whom they supposed themselves to be saving from Napoleon's grasp. Even more successfully than his father, Pitt made the English feel that they had a mighty mission, that if God had not given the world to them He had at least given them to the world.

The reality of Pitt's work undid much that his father had done. He exalted not only the office of prime minister but the whole structure of government: never again would independent men believe, as they had done when Chatham first fired them, that the liberties of Englishmen depended on unwinking hostility to central government and to all its administrative outworks. But the legend he had begotten, far more potent than

OPPOSITE A broadsheet in praise of Pitt.

AN INDEPENDENT TRIBUTE

To the Memory of

THE RIGHT HON. WILLIAM PITT.

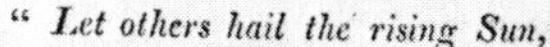

" Let others hail the rising Sun,
" I bow to that whose race is run."

By W. T. FITZGERALD, Esq.
January, 25, 1806.

SCARCE had the Tear that dew'd our NELSON'S Hearse,
Call'd forth The Tribute of each Patriot Verse,
When PITT, in Manhood's prime, resign'd his Breath,
And join'd The Hero of his Choice in Death.
Long had he stood The Atlas of The State,
By Men who lov'd him not---acknowledg'd Great!
Contending Parties charm'd! attentive hung,
On Tully's Periods flowing from his Tongue!
His Matchless Eloquence all Bosoms fir'd,
Which those who most oppos'd him, most admir'd,
His upright Breast pursued no selfish end,
At once The Monarch's, and The People's Friend!
And when he trusted to himself alone
He seldom err'd---his faults were not his own.
Through many a Civil Storm he firmly stood,
The object of his heart his Country's Good!
And 'till his Plans by Austria's Fate were cross'd,
The Liberties of Nations were not lost:
Amidst the Wreck, he saw This Island free,
Safe in her strength, and Sov'reign of The Sea.
Though plac'd where strong Temptations might allure,
The Minister of England still was Poor----
Do justice, BRITONS, to his spotless Mind,
Who govern'd Kingdoms, left no Wealth behind!

any reality, completed and even sanctified his father's work. He had given new meaning to Chatham's Patriot ideals, turning them into outward-looking and belligerent channels through which would eventually flow the full tide of Victorian imperialism. When his end came, at four o'clock in the morning of 23 January 1806, even his fiercest enemies felt the poorer for his passing. Already they sensed what their descendants were increasingly to feel: the enormous gulf between his limited and apparently clerkly talents and the great use to which he had put them. The Duchess of Devonshire, proudest of all Fox's aristocratic supporters, had said in 1784 that if Pitt prevailed 'he himself as well as every Englishman will repent ever after'. Now, at the news of his death, she could only marvel at his greatness. 'Poor Pitt died in the night,' she wrote. 'It is awful to the mind to reflect on a death of such magnitude, on the death of a man who had so long filled an immense space in the universe.' Even the most sceptical historian, puzzled though he may be as to how exactly the space was filled, cannot doubt its immensity.

BIBLIOGRAPHY

I PITT'S LETTERS AND SPEECHES

Since it has been found impossible to provide references in the form of footnotes I have tried wherever possible to give the dates of important letters and speeches, so that the reader can check them for himself if he wishes. There are many sources for Pitt's speeches, but for the sake of consistency I have taken all quotations from *The Parliamentary History of England*, published by William Cobbett between 1806 and 1820. Most of the letters about Pitt as a boy come from the *Chatham Correspondence*, eds., W.J.Taylor and J.H.Pringle, 4 vols 1838-40, though there is some additional material printed in Sir Tresham Lever, *The House of Pitt*, 1947. Earl Stanhope's *Life of Pitt*, 4 vols 1861-2, prints some of Pitt's letters to his mother and to his friends; it also includes, as a series of appendices, selections from his correspondence with the King. Further extracts from this were published in *Pitt and Napoleon, Essays and Letters*, by J. Holland Rose, 1912 and the remainder is in *The Later Correspondence of George III*, ed. A.Aspinall, 5 vols 1962-70. The originals of all these letters, as well as many other important Pitt papers, are in the Public Record Office in London (P.R.O.30/8/101–363); but relatively little of importance remains unpublished, except for private papers. The details of Pitt's wine bills, of his expenses at Goostree's and of his dinners at Downing Street come, for instance, from P.R.O.30/8/219, parts I and VI.

Details of Pitt papers other than those in the Public Record Office are given in J.Ehrman, *The Younger Pitt, the years of acclaim*, 1969, pp. 667–8. There is some important material in *Secret Correspondence connected with Mr Pitt's return to Office in 1804*, edited by Earl Stanhope and privately printed in 1852, and also in *Correspondence between William Pitt and Charles, Duke of Rutland, 1781–7*, edited by a later Earl Stanhope in 1890. The Grenville papers for this period are also of importance: some are in *Memoirs of the Courts and Cabinets of George III* by the Duke of Buckingham and Chandos (son of the third Earl Temple, Pitt's cousin and fellow conspirator in 1783), 4 vols 1853-5, but the great mass of them form the Dropmore collection and are calendared in series 30 of the Historical Manuscripts Commission Reports (HMC 30, *Fortescue* I–VII, 1792-1910). HMC 24, *Rutland* III, 1894, also has useful material on the early years of Pitt's ministry.

Letters and memoirs by Pitt's contemporaries which bear upon his career include: *The Journal and Correspondence of Lord Auckland*, 4 vols 1861-2; *The Correspondence of Edmund Burke*, eds. T.W.Copeland *et al.*, 9 vols 1958-70; *Memorials and Correspondence of Charles James Fox*, ed. Lord John Russell, 4 vols 1853-7; *The Correspondence of George, Prince of Wales, 1770-1812*, ed. A.Aspinall, 8 vols 1963-71; *Diaries and Correspondence of the Earl of Malmesbury*, 4 vols 1844; *Recollections of the Table Talk of Samuel Rogers*, ed. A.Dyce, 1887; *Life of Sir Samuel Romilly*, 3rd edition, 2 vols 1842; *Diaries and Correspondence of George Rose*, ed. L.V.Harcourt, 1860; *Diary of William Windham*, ed. Mrs Henry Baring, 1866; *Windham Papers*, ed. Earl of Rosebery, 2 vols 1913. *The Torrington Diaries* ed. C.B.Andrews, 4 vols 1934-8, and *The Farington Diary*, ed. James Greig, 8 vols 1922-8, are of interest for the background of public opinion, though neither is the work of an informed politician.

2 BIOGRAPHIES OF PITT

Bishop Tomline's *Memoirs of the life of William Pitt* (2 vols 1821, followed by a third privately printed for the Earl of Rosebery in 1903) was eagerly awaited, since Pitt had left his papers to Tomline, who had been his tutor; but in fact the discreet prelate destroyed many of the letters and produced a dull compilation of secondary sources. The first real biography – and still in many ways the best – was that by Earl Stanhope (see above, under Section 1). Macaulay's essay on Pitt, written in 1858, appeared at about the same time and has been reprinted many times and in many forms. It is still worth reading, as is Lord Rosebery's *Pitt*, first published in 1891. J.Holland Rose, *William Pitt and National Revival* and *William Pitt and the Great War*, both published in 1911, did much to popularise the picture of Pitt as the saviour of Europe from the tyrant Napoleon. D.G.Barnes, *George III and William Pitt*, 1938 (reprinted 1965) stressed Pitt's subservience to the King, while J.W.Derry, *William Pitt*, 1962, provided a readable and up-to-date sketch. J.Ehrman's scholarly and full treatment of the subject, with particular emphasis on the details of administrative history, promises to be definitive, but so far only one volume has appeared: *The Younger Pitt, the years of acclaim*, 1969.

3 FURTHER READING

General histories of the period include: Asa Briggs, *The Age of Improvement*, 1959; Derek Jarrett, *Britain 1688–1815*, 1965; J.H. Plumb, *England in the eighteenth century*, 1950; J.Steven Watson, *The Reign of George III*, 1960. The social history of these years has been much romanticised: for useful correctives see Dorothy George,

England in Transition, 1931 (revised ed., Penguin Books 1953); Dorothy Marshall, *English People in the eighteenth century*, 1956; P. Mathias, *The First Industrial Nation*, 1969; G.E. Mingay, *English Landed Society in the eighteenth century*, 1963; E.P. Thompson, *The Making of the English Working Class*, 1963. Derek Jarrett, *England in the Age of Hogarth*, 1974, provides a picture of English society from the 1730s to the 1790s.

On the politics of the 1780s see J. Cannon, *The Fox–North Coalition, 1782–4*, 1969; I.R. Christie, *The End of North's Ministry, 1780–2*, 1958 and *Wilkes, Wyvill and Reform*, 1962; J.W. Derry, *The Regency Crisis and the Whigs, 1788–9*; P.J. Marshall, *The Impeachment of Warren Hastings*, 1965; L.G. Mitchell, *Charles James Fox and the disintegration of the Whig Party, 1782–94*, 1971; J. Norris, *Shelburne and Reform*, 1963; L.S. Sutherland, *The East India Company in eighteenth century politics*, 1952. The history of the East India Company is carried into the 1790s in C.H. Philips, *The East India Company 1784–1833*, 2nd ed., 1961, while politics during the same period are dealt with in F. O'Gorman, *The Whig Party and the French Revolution*, 1967. P.A. Brown, *The French Revolution in English History*, 1918, is a classic work though rather dated, but G.S. Veitch, *The Genesis of Parliamentary Reform*, 1915, reprinted 1964, is still useful. The complex subject of England's involvement with France is dealt with in Derek Jarrett, *The Begetters of Revolution*, 1973, but this only goes up to 1789. Thomas Pakenham, *The Year of Liberty*, 1969, tells the story of the 1798 rebellion and J.C. Beckett, *The Making of Modern Ireland, 1603–1923*, 1966, gives a general account of Irish history. A. Cobban, *Ambassadors and Secret Agents*, 1954, provides a fascinating account of the Anglo-French struggle in the Dutch Republic in 1786-7, while Sir Arthur Bryant tells the story of Pitt's wars with France in dramatic and patriotic fashion in *The Years of Endurance 1793–1802*, 1942 and *The Years of Victory 1802–12*, 1944. For a calmer and more balanced view of French policy towards England from the 1790s onwards see P. Geyl, *Napoleon, For and Against*, 1949.

Among the biographies of Pitt's contemporaries John Brooke, *King George III*, 1972 is outstanding. S. Ayling, *George the Third*, 1972; J. Clarke, *The Life and Times of George III*, 1972; J.W. Derry, *Charles James Fox*, 1972; L. Reid, *Charles James Fox, a man for the people*, 1969; Oliver Warner, *William Wilberforce*, 1962; P. Ziegler, *Addington*, 1965 are also useful.

GENEALOGICAL TREE

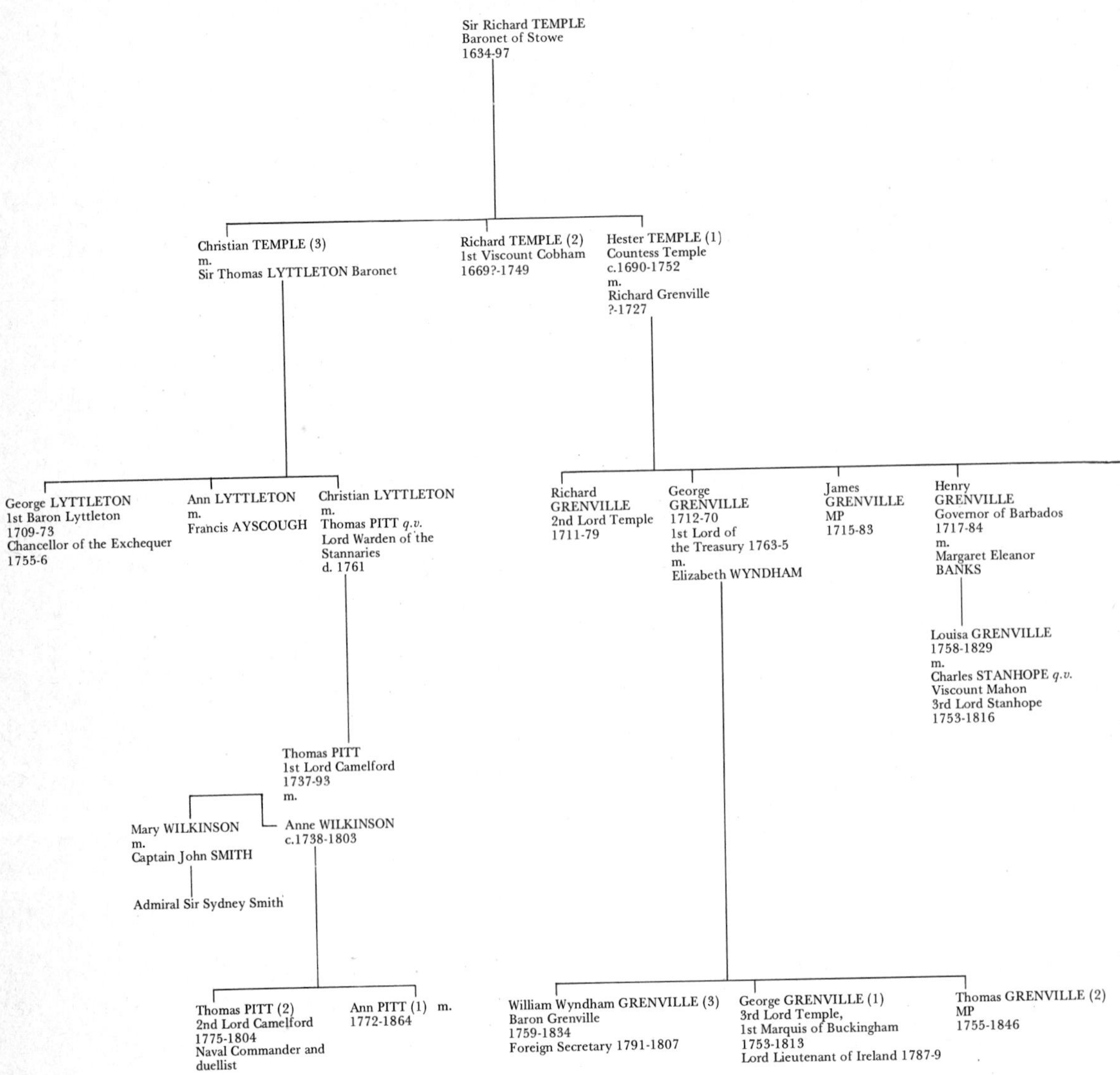

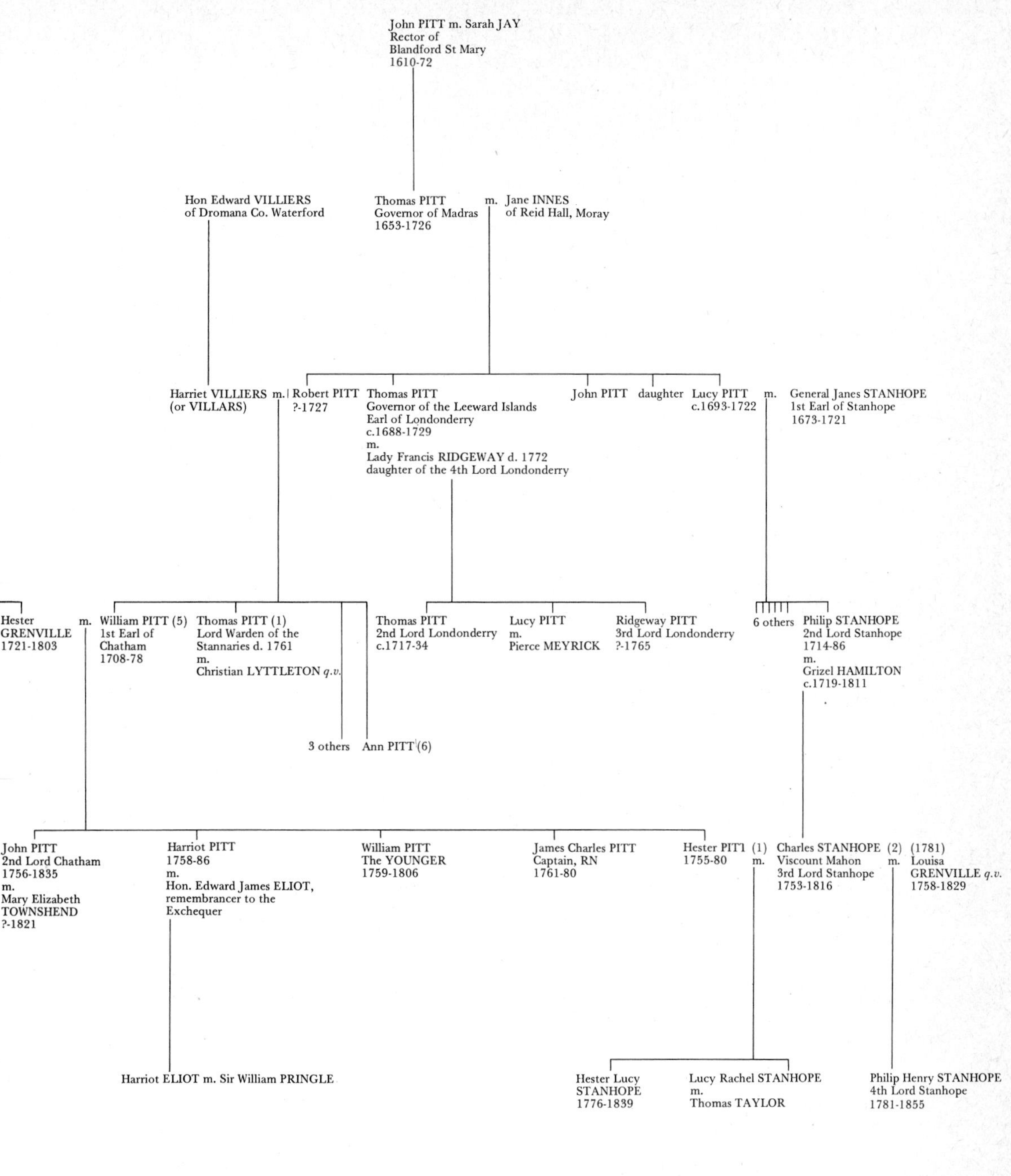

John PITT m. Sarah JAY
Rector of
Blandford St Mary
1610-72
Hon Edward VILLIERS
of Dromana Co. Waterford
Thomas PITT
Governor of Madras
1653-1726
m. Jane INNES
of Reid Hall, Moray
Harriet VILLIERS
(or VILLARS)
m.
Robert PITT
?-1727
Thomas PITT
Governor of the Leeward Islands
Earl of Londonderry
c.1688-1729
m.
Lady Francis RIDGEWAY d. 1772
daughter of the 4th Lord Londonderry
John PITT
daughter
Lucy PITT
c.1693-1722
m.
General Janes STANHOPE
1st Earl of Stanhope
1673-1721
Hester
GRENVILLE
1721-1803
m.
William PITT (5)
1st Earl of
Chatham
1708-78
Thomas PITT (1)
Lord Warden of the
Stannaries d. 1761
m.
Christian LYTTLETON q.v.
3 others
Ann PITT (6)
Thomas PITT
2nd Lord Londonderry
c.1717-34
Lucy PITT
m.
Pierce MEYRICK
Ridgeway PITT
3rd Lord Londonderry
?-1765
6 others
Philip STANHOPE
2nd Lord Stanhope
1714-86
m.
Grizel HAMILTON
c.1719-1811
John PITT
2nd Lord Chatham
1756-1835
m.
Mary Elizabeth
TOWNSHEND
?-1821
Harriot PITT
1758-86
m.
Hon. Edward James ELIOT,
remembrancer to the
Exchequer
William PITT
The YOUNGER
1759-1806
James Charles PITT
Captain, RN
1761-80
Hester PITT
1755-80
(1)
m.
Charles STANHOPE
Viscount Mahon
3rd Lord Stanhope
1753-1816
(2)
m.
(1781)
Louisa
GRENVILLE q.v.
1758-1829
Harriot ELIOT m. Sir William PRINGLE
Hester Lucy
STANHOPE
1776-1839
Lucy Rachel STANHOPE
m.
Thomas TAYLOR
Philip Henry STANHOPE
4th Lord Stanhope
1781-1855

INDEX

TREASURY
"To the Nuptial-Bower he led her, Blushing like the Morn." || The NUP